PATHWAYS
TO PEACE

The report was prepared with financial assistance from the Commission of the European Communities. The views expressed herein are those of the consultant and do not represent any official view of the Commission.

The Royal Institute of International Affairs is an independent body which promotes the rigorous study of international questions and does not express opinions of its own. The opinions expressed in this publication are the responsibility of the author.

PATHWAYS TO PEACE

The Multilateral Arab–Israeli Peace Talks

Joel Peters

EUROPEAN
COMMISSION

RIIA

© Royal Institute of International Affairs, 1996

Published in Great Britain in 1996 by the Royal Institute of International Affairs,
Chatham House, 10 St James's Square, London SW1Y 4LE
(Charity Registration No. 208 223).

Distributed worldwide by The Brookings Institution, 1775 Massachusetts Avenue, NW,
Washington, DC 20036-2188, USA.

British Library Cataloguing in Publication Data
A CIP catalogue record for this book is available from the British Library.

ISBN 1 899658 15 7

Text set in Bembo.
Printed and bound in Great Britain by Biddles Limited, Guildford and King's Lynn.

To all those who have sung
a song for peace

CONTENTS

ACKNOWLEDGMENTS

Numerous people have helped me greatly in the research and writing of this book. My thanks must go first of all to my colleagues in the Middle East Programme at the Royal Institute of International Affairs who, over the years, have supported and assisted my work in a variety of ways. I would like to thank Dr Philip Robins, formerly the head of the programme and now of St Antony's College, Oxford, who first suggested that I work on this subject, and Dr Rosemary Hollis, the current programme head, for their continual support. Jill Devey and Valerie Grove have been responsible for administering this project at various points with a great amount of energy, patience and humour, ensuring its successful completion. I am grateful to Margaret May and Hannah Doe of the RIIA Publications Department, as well as Gillian Bromley, for their help and work on the editorial and production side of the publication.

I would also like to thank my colleagues in the Department of Politics at the University of Reading for all their encouragement, and the University of Reading Research Endowment Fund for awarding me a grant to carry out research on the Arab–Israeli peace process.

I am indebted to the Directorate-General for South Mediterranean, Near and Middle East (DG1B/A) of the European Commission for their financial and personal support of my research on the multilateral talks. Charles Alexis-Mossa, in particular, has been especially generous with his time and encouragement of my work.

Over the past couple of years a series of research trips have been made to Jerusalem, the West Bank and Gaza, Amman, Cairo, Washington and the European Commission in Brussels in order to collect material and conduct interviews with officials involved in the multilateral talks. I would like to acknowledge all the American, Canadian, Egyptian,

European, Israeli, Japanese, Jordanian and Palestinian officials who have spent numerous hours informing, clarifying and correcting my ideas on these talks. Simply put, this book would have been impossible without their assistance. Some will recognize their thoughts in these pages; others will disagree with my conclusions. None, however, are responsible for the ideas contained in this study. The book has also benefited from a number of study groups and a two-day workshop held at Chatham House in June 1995. I am grateful to everyone who commented on earlier drafts and participated in those meetings.

Numerous friends and colleagues have heard more about the multilaterals than they thought possible, but have listened without (too much) complaint. They will be as glad as I that it is finally finished. Anne Wilstead, Alan Barber and Vikki Lloyd have provided valuable research assistance at various times. Jorge Grunberg has been a loyal ally and Bruce Hurwitz has cheered me on from afar. Special thanks must go to Raymond Cohen who has been, as ever, a continual source of friendship, encouragement and ideas.

This study has been written at a time of dramatic change and hope in the Middle East. Its aim is to promote a greater understanding and awareness of the multilateral talks and of their contribution to the building of a new set of peaceful relations between Israel and the Arab world. It is dedicated to the memory of my father, who guided me along my own path, and to all those who have sung a song for peace. Any credit that I may receive I would like to share with my friends who have helped me along the way. Its faults, as always, are mine alone.

January 1996   Joel Peters

ABOUT THE AUTHOR

Dr Joel Peters is Lecturer in International Relations in the Department of Politics and Director of International Studies in the Graduate School of European and International Studies at the University of Reading. He is an Associate Research Fellow of the Middle East Programme at the Royal Institute of International Affairs, London.

He is the author of *Israel and Africa: The Problematic Friendship* (London: British Academic Press, 1992) and an RIIA Special Paper *Building Bridges: The Multilateral Arab–Israeli Peace Talks* (1994) and co-editor (with Keith Kyle) of *Whither Israel: The Domestic Challenges* (London: I.B. Tauris/Royal Institute of International Affairs, 1994).

Dr Peters gained his Bsc (Econ.) in International Relations at the London School of Economics and received his doctorate in International Relations from the University of Oxford, where he studied at St Antony's College.

He has been a visiting scholar at the Center for African Studies and the Center for International and Strategic Affairs at the University of California, Los Angeles, and at the Department of International Relations and the Harry S. Truman Institute for the Advancement of Peace, both at the Hebrew University, Jerusalem.

1 INTRODUCTION

Developments in recent years have led to a wave of optimism that the Middle East is on the verge of new era of cooperation and peace. A comprehensive resolution to the Arab–Israeli conflict appears at last to be a real rather than an imaginary prospect. For the better part of two years, following the Madrid peace conference of October 1991, Israel, Syria, Lebanon, Jordan and the Palestinians had found themselves trapped in a series of painstaking negotiations in Washington that seemed to be leading nowhere. It was the dramatic revelation in August 1993 that Israel and the Palestine Liberation Organization (PLO) had been negotiating secretly in Oslo, well away from the official process which had grown out of the Madrid conference, and that they had reached agreement on an interim accord over limited self-government for the Gaza Strip and Jericho, that was to transform the Arab–Israeli peace process.

The signing of the Israeli–Palestinian Declaration of Principles in September 1993, marked by the memorable handshake on the White House lawn, spawned a series of further breakthroughs between Israel and its Arab neighbours. In May 1994 Israel and the PLO signed the Gaza–Jericho accord, resulting in Israeli withdrawal from those areas, and the transfer of civilian powers to the Palestinians there. This was followed by the signing in September 1995 of the 'Oslo II' interim agreement leading to the redeployment of Israeli forces away from the major centres of population in the West Bank and the holding of elections on 20 January 1996 for a Palestinian Council. The breakthrough between Israel and the Palestinians was the catalyst for Israel and Jordan to put aside their differences and sign a full peace treaty on 26 October 1994. Since that point diplomatic relations between the two countries, spurred on by the public resolve displayed by their leaders, have flourished.

Negotiations between Israel and Syria have proved to be far more problematic. However, at the end of 1995 talks between the two countries were resumed in Washington at a higher level of representation than before and with a degree of expectancy and commitment not previously witnessed. The willingness of Morocco and Tunisia and the Gulf states – most notably Oman and Qatar – to engage in an open dialogue with Israel, and the progressive withering away of the Arab economic boycott of that country, are further signs that a major turning point in the history of the Arab–Israeli conflict has been reached. The peace process has a long way still to travel and its opponents cannot be lightly discounted, as the tragic assassination of Israel's Prime Minister Yitzhak Rabin so dramatically reminded the world. Nonetheless, the search for a comprehensive, just and lasting peace between Israel and the Arab world has now become deeply embedded in the international politics of the Middle East.

The peace process has focused primarily on the political issues that lie at the heart of the Arab–Israeli conflict, namely territorial withdrawal, border demarcation, security arrangements and the political rights of the Palestinians. Peace will only be sustainable, however, if the peace agreements, once concluded, are coupled with a long-term cooperation process involving all states of the region. This requires Israel and the Arab states to lay aside their old animosities and fears in order to establish new patterns of behaviour and to think creatively about new institutional mechanisms to underpin those activities. Further, it demands not only the commitment of the regional parties but also the active support of the international community to sustain those endeavours.

The architects of the current peace process, which opened with the Madrid conference of October 1991, recognized the need to address simultaneously the economic, social and environmental problems which cut across national boundaries. To this end they created a set of multilateral talks to run in parallel with the bilateral negotiations. The aim was to bring together Israel, its immediate Arab neighbours and the wider circle of Arab states in the Gulf and the Maghreb to discuss issues of regional concern within a framework for dealing with issues of mutual interest which might also serve as confidence-building measures and facilitate progress at the bilateral level. The multilateral talks have been formally under way since the inaugural organizational meeting in Moscow in January 1992. Since then the participants have met for seven rounds of talks in five separate working groups to discuss water resources, environmental issues, refugees, arms control and regional security, and economic and regional development. Yet despite the fact that the multilaterals are an integral part of the peace process, little is known about them. Press coverage has been meagre, public interest muted. As a result there is little awareness of the nature of these talks, of how the meetings operate, or of the agendas and issues under discussion. A clear understanding of the dynamics and the content of the multilateral talks has been confined to a small group of diplomats.

This absence of attention should not, however, be taken to indicate a lack of progress. On the contrary, these talks, hidden away from the glare of international media coverage, have generated a series of significant developments over the past four years. The multilaterals have given rise to a wide agenda of projects and joint ventures and have provided a unique forum for communication between Israel and the Arabs. The scepticism that first greeted the multilateral track has recently receded, to be replaced by a wave of cautious optimism. Recognition of the importance of the regional component in the peace process has been gaining steadily in currency. Few in 1992, including the architects of the talks and those present at the opening meeting in Moscow in January of that year, would have envisioned the developments and successes since achieved in this arena, especially in the light of the difficulties encountered in the bilateral negotiations over the same period.

The relative inattention to the multilateral track has been accompanied by a poverty in the analysis of the role and contribution of these talks. The aim of this study is to promote the academic discussion and raise the level of public awareness of this aspect of the peace process. The book falls into three parts. Chapter 2 examines the aims, structure and operating procedures of the talks. Chapters 3–8 highlight the issues under discussion and the activities in the Steering Group and in each of the five working groups. Chapter 9 evaluates the role of the multilateral talks in the Arab–Israeli peace process and the contribution they have made, and concludes with a number of observations about the future role, functioning and management of the multilateral track.

A stock-taking exercise of this kind, arriving at a clearer understanding of these talks, is of particular value in that it may illuminate their contribution to the quest to go beyond bilateral agreements to end the state of belligerency and achieve a more comprehensive resolution of the Arab–Israeli conflict and build a new era of regional cooperation in the Middle East. In so doing it is to be hoped that this study can point the way to further progress in this regard.

2 ORIGINS, AIMS AND STRUCTURE OF THE MULTILATERAL TALKS

Origins and aims

The multilateral talks were devised with two broad aims in view. In part the intention was to facilitate progress at the bilateral level by creating a separate arena in which Israel, its immediate Arab neighbours and the wider circle of Arab states in the Gulf and the Maghreb could discuss what are technically considered non-political issues of mutual concern in such a way that developments in these areas would serve as confidence-building measures between the parties. In part the objective was that the multilateral talks would make progress in their own right, in the interests of addressing region-wide problems at a regional level. The involvement of the international community in the talks, meanwhile, brought benefits on both counts.

While the bilateral talks were to concentrate on the political issues of territorial control and sovereignty, border demarcations, security arrangements and the political rights of the Palestinians, the multilaterals, as envisaged, would examine a range of primarily non-political issues which extend across national boundaries, and the resolution of which is essential for the promotion of long-term regional development and security. Whereas the bilaterals would deal with the problems inherited from the past, the multilaterals would focus on the future shape of the Middle East. The need for cooperative arrangements to foster economic development, to preserve and enhance the supply of water, and to control environmental degradation is shared by all the states in the region. Many of these issues do not demand, nor can they wait for, a comprehensive and final settlement to the Arab–Israeli conflict.

The idea of the multilateral track is grounded in a functionalist view of international cooperation and peace according to which the enmeshing of the states in the region in an ever-widening web of economic, technical and welfare interdependencies would force them to set aside their political and/ or ideological rivalries. The process of continuing cooperation in areas of mutual concern would blur long-held animosities and would create a new perception of shared needs. Continuous interaction would be accompanied by a learning process which would foster a fundamental change in attitudes and lead to a convergence of expectations and the institutionalization of norms of behaviour. From progress in the multilaterals would emerge a vision of what real peace might entail and the benefits that would accrue to all parties, thereby facilitating progress in the bilateral talks. Functional cooperation would eventually spill over into regional peace.

At the same time the addition of the multilateral track was driven by practical considerations. While the principal purpose was to bring together the regional parties, a secondary consideration was to draw the international community, which had been effectively excluded from the sponsorship of the Madrid conference and the substantive issues under discussion in the bilateral negotiations, into the peace process. The regional dimension of peace and security, in all its aspects, is essential for the long-term durability of any Arab–Israeli settlement. This requires not only the sustained commitment of the regional parties themselves but also the active support of the international community. Thus, the multilaterals were designed to marshal the expertise, experience and, above all, the financial resources of the international community to secure the foundations for a lasting and comprehensive settlement to the Arab–Israeli conflict.

The thinking behind initiation of the talks was outlined by the then US Secretary of State James Baker in his opening remarks to the organizational meeting in Moscow in January 1992:

> It is for these reasons that we have come together – to address those issues that are common to the region and that do not necessarily respect national boundaries or geographic boundaries. These issues can be best addressed by the concerted efforts of the regional parties together with the support of the international community and the resources and expertise that it can provide.
>
> … What we are embarking upon here in Moscow is in no way a substitute for what we are trying to promote in the bilateral negotiations.

Only the bilateral talks can address and one day resolve the basic issues of territory, security and peace which the parties have identified as the core elements of a lasting and comprehensive peace between Israel and its neighbours.

But it is true that these bilateral negotiations do not take place in a vacuum, and that the condition of the region at large will affect them. In short, the multilateral talks are intended as a complement to the bilateral negotiations: each can and will buttress the other.

One of the hopes implicit in US logic was to send a powerful signal that all the participants, regional and non-regional alike, were fully committed to the ending of the Arab–Israeli conflict and to the building of a new set of peaceful and cooperative relations between Israel and the Arab world. In fact, the addition of the multilateral track to the Madrid process by the United States was an ambitious undertaking and not without risk. The widening of the peace process was dismissed by many as a way of placating Israel and ensuring its participation at the Madrid conference. Bringing together Israel and all the Arab states of the region to discuss problems of mutual concern and areas of future cooperation prior to the resolution of the core issues of the Arab–Israeli conflict appeared to be not only idealistic but naive. There was a perceived danger that, instead of serving as a forum for constructive dialogue, the multilaterals would be used as a platform for protest and polemic. Failure in these talks would have a negative impact on the peace process and would function as a confidence-destroying rather than a confidence-building exercise.

Few actually had any precise expectations of what tangible benefits might emerge from these talks. The lack of clarity in defining the specific questions that they would address and the vagueness of the relationship between the multilateral and the bilateral tracks raised serious questions about the value of the exercise. The three-month delay between the Madrid conference and the convening of the opening session in Moscow, together with the lack of real preparation by the participants for that meeting, only served to underline these doubts. However, the fears that the multilaterals would quickly collapse in acrimony and disarray proved to be unjustified.

Structure of the multilateral talks

When the opening session of the multilateral talks was held in Moscow at the end of January 1992, invitations were issued by the co-sponsors of the peace process, the United States and Russia, to Lebanon, Syria, Jordan, the Palestinians (under the aegis of a joint Palestinian/Jordanian delegation, as provided for in the Madrid formula), Israel, Egypt, Algeria, Tunisia, Morocco, Mauritania, Saudi Arabia, Kuwait, Bahrain, the United Arab Emirates, Qatar, Oman, Yemen, the European Community (to be represented at the ministerial level by the EC Presidency and the European Commission), Turkey, Canada, a representative of the EFTA countries, Japan and China. The proceedings were boycotted by Syria and Lebanon, which have regarded these talks as premature and, despite constant appeals by all the parties concerned to join this process, have consistently refused to attend any of the multilateral gatherings, arguing that the Arab states should not discuss matters of regional cooperation with Israel until a political settlement is reached at the bilateral level. Syria, in particular, has been vehement in denouncing these talks and has urged the Arab states to reconsider their participation as an additional means of pressurizing Israel into making concessions and withdrawing from the occupied territories.[1] A Palestinian delegation arrived in Moscow but did not formally attend the opening session, arguing that the Madrid formula which excluded Palestinians from outside the occupied territories should not apply to the multilateral framework. In contrast to Syria and Lebanon, however, the Palestinians have participated in all five working groups, although they were not invited to join the arms control talks until the third round in May 1993. In October 1992 the new Labour-led coalition in Israel reversed the policy of its predecessor government and agreed that Palestinian delegates from the diaspora should be allowed to attend these meetings provided that they were not members of the PLO or the Palestine National Council (PNC).

In contrast to the detailed preparation and strenuous diplomatic efforts that marked the Madrid conference and the bilateral negotiations in Washington, great uncertainty surrounded the opening multilateral meeting in Moscow. Beyond the broader goals of this track, there was little idea of what specific issues would be addressed in this forum, how the meetings would be conducted and how the process would be managed. Unlike the Conference on Security and Cooperation in Europe (CSCE), which was preceded by six months of preparatory talks (the so-called Helsinki consultations), no clear guidelines, institutional arrangements or rules of procedure were drawn up beforehand. However, from this shaky foundation a sense of meaning and direction has developed, and a recognizable pattern, structure and set of procedural modalities has emerged. The multilateral track has generated its own dynamics, language, rules and procedures.

The Steering Group

At the apex of the multilaterals stands the Steering Group, which meets at the conclusion of each round of talks. The primary role of the Steering Group is to oversee the activities of the working groups and to effect any changes in the structure, composition and operating procedures of the whole multilateral track. The Steering Group operates, as do all meetings within the framework of the multilaterals, according to the principle of consensus and not that of majority voting. The use of consensus as a mode of decision-making in multilateral gatherings has become increasingly prevalent and is regarded as an important technique for the achievement of agreement in international negotiations. The term has come to mean that none of the participants opposes the agreements or outcomes reached, although the degree of support for any agreement may well vary.[2] The consensus approach encourages the breaking down of issues into more manageable components and the search for incremental agreements rather than an attempt to solve all aspects of a complex problem within one framework. The need for consensus means that outcomes initially reflect the lowest common denominator in areas of concern among the parties, while the more contentious issues are deferred to the later stages of the negotiating process. It is from the ability to veto issues that states derive their bargaining power in multilateral negotiations. The consensus approach assures the introduction of an element of formal egalitarianism into the proceedings. From the Israeli perspective, this has meant that the agenda for the multilateral talks has not been dominated by the Arab states as a result of their numerical superiority. From the perspective of the Arab states, on the other hand, the requirement of consensus has allowed Israel, with the tacit support of the United States, to dictate the running of these talks and prevent the introduction of certain issues.

The working groups

The multilateral talks comprise five working groups, on water resources, environment, refugees, arms control and regional security, and regional economic development. Each of the five groups has met for seven rounds of talks since the convening of the opening meeting in Moscow.[3] (For the dates and location of these meetings see Appendix 2.) The fact that these groups meet simultaneously and that they are referred to collectively under the rubric of the multilateral talks conveys the impression of unity and complementarity. In practice, however, the working groups differ significantly in their internal dynamics, in their composition and in the level of progress achieved over the past four years. There is little coordination between the groups, and developments in one set of talks have not resulted in any immediate spill-over effect.

Since the working groups operate under the consensus system of decision-making, the sessions have been designed to allow the parties to raise issues and concerns without entering into adversarial bargaining positions. Emphasis has been placed on loose, informal frameworks and consensual bargains. No official minutes of the proceedings have been recorded, and the parties have been careful to avoid making the drafting of reports and formal statements a primary focus. At the conclusion of each meeting the gavel-holder (see below) produces a short statement outlining in brief the nature of the discussions and the principal issues raised in the meeting. These statements serve as the basis of the gavel-holders' reports to the Steering Group; they are not regarded as formal binding documents. Even so, the drafting of these statements has not always been a simple task and has entailed quiet negotiations of compromises and trade-offs in the corridors outside the main hall, as well as resort to deliberately imprecise and ambiguous wording.

The gavel-holder

The multilaterals have developed a specific terminology to describe the various functions and activities which to the outside observer can appear obscure and confusing. Each working group is run by a gavel-holder, who is assisted in this task by two or three co-organizers. The term 'gavel-holder' was chosen to convey a neutral, passive role, signifying someone who ensures the smooth running of a meeting and exerts authority only if discussions become too disorderly. In fact, the term is a misnomer since the role of gavel-holders has extended way beyond merely presiding over the plenary sessions. They have undertaken many of the traditional tasks involved in the chairing of multilateral gatherings, such as defining the agendas for the meetings, preparing documentation, mediating quietly, when necessary, between the parties, drafting the closing remarks and coordinating the running of the inter-sessional activities.

The inter-sessionals

The real work of the multilaterals, especially since the third round, has been conducted not in the plenary meetings of the working groups but in the 'inter-sessionals' which occur between the meetings. This term covers a vast range of activities, from joint visits and workshops to the preparation of feasibility studies for various projects.

The shepherds

The various inter-sessional activities are organized primarily by the extra-regional parties, who act as 'shepherds' for these projects and have taken on the responsibility for directing these activities. The idea of a 'shepherd' conjures up a mixed set of images. Often a shepherd is seen as sitting on the sidelines quietly supervising his flock. However, his flock will only move forward once it has been pushed in the right direction. It is the second of these images that best conveys the role of the 'shepherds' in the multilateral talks. The extra-regional parties have played a critical role in promoting the various activities agreed upon in the working groups. The degree of success and progress evident in the numerous projects has been a direct outcome of the commitment, effort and resources offered by the international community in their support.

3 THE STEERING GROUP

Representative of the key players in the multilaterals, the Steering Group comprises the co-sponsors (the United States and Russia); the bilateral negotiating parties, that is Israel, Egypt, Jordan, the Palestinians, Saudi Arabia (representing the Gulf Cooperation Council, GCC) and Tunisia (representing the Arab Maghreb Union, UMA); and the European Union, Japan and Canada as lead organizers of the working groups. In December 1993 Norway, as chair of the Ad Hoc Liaison Committee, was invited to join the Steering Group.[1] Places have also been reserved for Syria and Lebanon should they decide to join the multilateral talks. The Steering Group has met six times at the conclusion of each round of the multilateral working groups. It has also held two inter-sessional meetings. (For the dates and locations of these meetings see Appendix 2.)

Although the Steering Group is the supreme body in the multilaterals, in fact it has effected few decisions and has performed, especially during the first four rounds, an essentially passive, ceremonial role. At each of those meetings the gavel-holders of the working groups merely presented oral summaries of the accomplishments and developments in their respective groups. The Steering Group confined itself to acknowledging receipt of those reports, determining the location and dates for the following round of talks and approving new participants in the working groups. The parties have refrained from allowing the Steering Group to play a more proactive role in guiding the pace or direction of the working groups or to alter either the architecture or the operating procedures of the talks. Proposals for the creation of additional groups to deal with energy, human rights, public health and Jerusalem have yet to achieve the necessary level of consensual support within the Steering Group. Nor has the request by the Arab states that the United Nations be offered a seat on the Steering Group been accepted.

By the end of the fourth round, the need to create a more systematic process for monitoring and coordinating the activities of the working groups was becoming increasingly apparent. In recognition of this fact, a preliminary discussion was held at the meeting in Tokyo on the future of the multilateral talks and on what role the Steering Group should play in directing the process. The parties were also encouraged to air their views on the overall long-term objectives of the talks.[2] These discussions were inconclusive and did not result in the adoption of any new concrete measures. The participants did, however, agree on the importance of reviewing the role of the Steering Group and decided to hold an inter-sessional meeting in Montebello at the beginning of February 1994 to develop their ideas.

The Montebello meeting marked a turning point in the history of the multilaterals as well as in the role of the Steering Group. For the first time the parties acknowledged the need for the Steering Group to provide leadership and a sense of strategic direction to the multilateral process. After a thorough review of the operating procedures of the multilaterals, the Steering Group drew up an action plan to guide the future activities of the five working groups. Specifically, it called upon the working groups to adopt, at their next meeting, a number of signature projects that could be implemented quickly and that would bring visible immediate benefits to the peoples of the region.

The Steering Group also demanded from the gavel–holders a greater degree of coordination, accountability and follow-up in the activities undertaken by the 'shepherds'. The gavel-holders were instructed to submit a report to the Steering Group following each plenary session outlining the principal achievements of their working group and the obstacles to further progress. These reports should include a summary of the discussions and a detailed overview of the decisions taken. Having hitherto gone to great lengths to keep the multilaterals out of the media limelight, the Steering Group now felt that the time was ripe to raise the public profile and widen the audience for these talks. The parties were accordingly encouraged to develop a greater role for and involvement of the private sector in their activities.

There was also a recognition that the multilateral track should not be concerned solely with the accumulation of projects, that it needed to develop a strategic vision and a set of principles for the Middle East. As a first step in this task the co-sponsors produced for discussion draft 'Guidelines for the Middle East Multilateral Peace Process'. It was also decided that the Steering Group would produce a paper on the future of the region. The drafting of these two documents is the principal task which the Steering Group has set itself. A considerable part of the proceedings of the plenary session in Tabarka, following the completion of the fifth round, was devoted to this subject. After an extensive debate, the Steering Group decided that the co-sponsors would produce a new draft of the guidelines paper which would be circulated to all the parties and be reviewed at a further inter-sessional meeting during the winter in the hope that it would be approved at the next plenary meeting of the Steering Group. A detailed work plan was also drawn up for the paper on the future of the region. While the co-sponsors would also be responsible for overseeing the drafting of this document, the gavel-holders agreed, somewhat unenthusiastically, to produce, in consultation with the regional parties, 'vision papers' in their areas of responsibility. At the inter-sessional meeting held in Cairo in January 1995 some headway was made in the redrafting of the guidelines, but no consensus could be reached over clauses regarding Jerusalem, the question of self-determination for the Palestinians and regional arms control arrangements.

The drafting of the guidelines and a discussion of the vision papers produced by the gavel-holders were originally intended to be the principal items on the agenda of the Steering Group meeting in Montreux in May 1995. However, following Israel's decision to expropriate more land in Jerusalem and the discussions in the US Congress on transferring the US embassy there from Tel Aviv, the future status of Jerusalem dominated the proceedings. The Arab states, led by the Palestinians, argued forcefully for the setting up of a new multilateral working group devoted exclusively to the question of Jerusalem.[3] Israel, clearly on the defensive and angered at the introduction of this issue onto the agenda, insisted that the multilaterals were not the appropriate forum for its discussion and refused to accede to this demand.[4] Discussions on the guidelines and on the vision papers were sidelined by the Jerusalem question, and the meeting concluded with no real clarity about either the overall purpose of the exercise or how best to proceed further.

The Montreux meeting was notable, however, for agreeing to address, for the first time, the issue of human rights within the multilateral track. Earlier suggestions for the inclusion of a separate working group on human rights had been flatly rejected by both Israel and the Arabs. In Montreux, Switzerland reintroduced this idea under the thinly disguised veil of a working group in the field of 'civil, political, social, economic and cultural rights and intercultural understanding'. The Steering Group felt that a separate working group was still premature, but entrusted the Swiss to act as shepherd for these issues within the framework of the existing working groups and to advise the co-sponsors on the human rights dimension of the multilateral process. In the light of the previous reluctance of both Israel and the Arabs to discuss human rights, the acceptance of the Swiss initiative, albeit in a diluted form, reflects the robustness and maturity of the multilateral track and a growing confidence in the peace process on the part of all the parties concerned.

4 THE WORKING GROUP ON WATER RESOURCES

> It appears equally clear that along with other outstanding issues of the
> Palestine dispute – compensation, repatriation, Jerusalem, boundaries –
> there is a fifth element, water, which must be considered as we approach a
> final settlement. (US Department of State Position Paper, 4 May 1953)[1]

In the arid, drought-prone conditions of the Middle East cooperation
over the management, enhancement and sharing of water resources ought
to be an area of mutual interest to all the parties in the region. Hitherto,
however, the need for water has not drawn states together into cooperative arrangements: instead, competition over water has been a source of
conflict in the Middle East. From its inception, the riparian dispute over
access to the water resources of the Jordan basin has been an integral
element of the Arab–Israeli conflict. Reflecting the importance of this
scarce resource and its potential as a focus for future conflict, the issue of
water has figured prominently in the bilateral negotiations and has been
accorded its own working group in the multilateral talks.[2]

The United States acts as the gavel-holder for this working group,
with the European Union and Japan serving as co-organizers. The group
has met seven times, most recently in a 'clustered' meeting with the
working group on the environment in Amman in June 1995 (for other
dates and locations see Appendix 2). Although all the parties have
recognized that levels of water wastage in the region are high, that the
supply of water does not match the ever-increasing demand and that
water quality has been deteriorating, the concrete results arising from the
activities of this working group have been limited. Nonetheless a number
of specific achievements can be identified, a wealth of expertise and
information has been mobilized and the parties have begun to focus on

the steps required to enhance and effectively manage the scarce water resources of the region.

From the outset, the running of this group has been fraught with a number of difficulties and political obstacles. Most notably, the absence of Syria and Lebanon from the talks has effectively limited the number of areas of potential cooperation and thwarted hopes that full and all-encompassing cooperation among the riparian states of the Jordan basin would be developed within this working group. In addition, the varying concerns of the regional participants and their differing expectations of this process have burdened the discussions and impeded greater breakthroughs. In particular, much of the discussion, especially in the early rounds, floundered over the inclusion of water rights as an agenda item. Israel has sought to separate the technical and political aspects of the water issue, regarding the primary objective of this working group as to focus solely on technical issues and joint water management, with the aim of increasing the overall supply of water within the region. The formulation of solutions to the problems of water supply, in the Israeli view, requires the development of a range of functional and technical links between regional experts and officials. The construction of these links should not be impeded by the discussion of water rights and shares which, for Israel, is essentially a political issue and therefore should be confined to the bilateral negotiations. To the chagrin of the Israelis, the Arab states – most notably Jordan and the Palestinians – were determined to address this question within the framework of the multilaterals. They regarded the consideration of water rights as a precondition to cooperation and pivotal to regional water management.[3]

The initial experience of the Working Group on Water Resources underscores the difficulty of separating the 'low politics' of the functional issues surrounding the use of water from the 'high politics' of the Arab–Israeli conflict. After all, water is not the only issue at stake in the riparian dispute: territorial and sovereignty rights are also involved. Thus progress towards finding solutions to the problem of water at the multilateral level will inevitably remain problematic until a positive resolution of the political conflict is secured.[4]

The sharp differences between Israel and the Arabs over the issue of water rights dominated the first three rounds of talks in this group and in

Geneva in April 1993 almost brought them to a halt. It was only following quiet negotiations held in May, prior to the meeting of the refugee working group in Oslo, that some of the main differences between Israel and the Palestinians were resolved. In a document signed by the two parties Israel agreed to the setting up of a working group in the bilateral negotiations to discuss the issue of water rights, and in return the Palestinians withdrew their threat to boycott the inter-sessional activities of the water group. However, even during the fourth round of talks in Beijing, and despite the inclusion of the question of water rights in the Declaration of Principles and the agenda drawn up by Israel and Jordan, this issue continued to permeate many of the discussions.

Some progress has been achieved despite fundamental differences, essentially because the Israeli position on the appropriate fora for the discussion of water rights has prevailed. The water working group has confined its activities to developing strategies for managing and increasing the supply of water in the region, and has concentrated its efforts on 'identifying the appropriate methods to supply adequate water to growing populations at an affordable cost'. To this end, the parties have focused upon four broad themes, adopted at the first plenary meeting in Vienna, as the starting points for discussion and potential cooperation: (1) enhancement of data availability; (2) water management and conservation; (3) enhancement of water supply; and (4) concepts of regional cooperation and management. In the course of these talks, the parties have become increasingly aware of the need to translate their deliberations into identifiable achievements and move towards the implementation of specific projects. Accordingly, at the 1994 meeting in Oman they endorsed five specific proposals as signature projects for the working group. These are:

- a German proposal for a study of supply and demand of the water needs of the interested core regional parties;
- an American proposal to develop waste-water treatment and reuse facilities for small communities at several sites in the Middle East;
- an Israeli proposal to rehabilitate municipal water supply systems in the region;
- an Omani proposal to establish a desalination research and technology centre in Muscat;

• the implementation of a regional training programme, sponsored by the Unites States and the European Union, for water officials and experts.

The working group has also adopted the practice, first initiated by the Working Group on the Environment, of holding a number of informal sessions during the plenary meetings to allow the delegates to discuss specific areas of cooperation in greater depth. Each of these sessions has concentrated on one of the projects adopted in each of the four agenda items: the plan for regional data banks; the project to rehabilitate municipal water supply systems, and the proposal to develop waste-water treatment and reuse facilities; the regional desalination research centre; and the regional training programme.

Enhancement of data availability

The availability of reliable and standardized water data is an essential prerequisite for any future cooperation among the parties over water resources in the region. Water planners and officials require access to shared and verifiable data on which to base the projections of future needs and water management practices. The regional parties have acknowledged the need for enhanced and improved data.

At the meeting in Beijing, they agreed that the setting up of a regional data bank to increase the availability and to facilitate the exchange of water data among the parties in the region should be one of the goals of the working group. Several inter-sessional activities were identified with this goal in mind, including a US–EU proposal for a visit by a team of experts to consult on data collection issues, a study tour of river basins in France, and a workshop on the standardization of methodologies and formats for data collection. It was also decided to initiate a hydrological mapping of the sources of the Jordan river.

At the meeting in Athens, the regional parties took a further step towards the achievement of this goal with the setting up of an Executive Action Team (EXACT) composed of Israeli, Jordanian and Palestinian water officials. This team has met several times in the region and has produced a detailed plan for the upgrading and standardizing of water data collection by all three parties. The regional parties, with the support of the United States, the European Union, Canada and France, which have all offered financial support for the work of EXACT, are currently implementing specific elements of the plan.

Water management and conservation

The water resources working group has approved several projects aimed at improving water management and conservation practices in the region. A number of studies have been commissioned and a variety of workshops have been organized.

At the meeting in Oman, the group approved an Israeli project – the first time that an Israeli proposal had been endorsed by any of the five working groups – for the rehabilitation and more efficient use of municipal water supply systems in the region. This initiative formed part of a broader package of small projects for immediate implementation and development (SPIID) presented by Israel to the meeting. The aim of the project is to identify the sources of, and thereby reduce, water losses as a result of leakages and deficiencies (inadequate piping and pumping) in the existing supply systems of a number of specific medium-sized communities in the region.

As a significant amount of water is used for agriculture, a number of projects have focused on improving methods of irrigation in the region. Austria is shepherding a project looking at the usage of marginal water for irrigation, while Luxembourg is heading a study of potential ways of maximizing revenues through intensive agriculture in Gaza under varying water conditions.

Other projects undertaken by the group in this area include a study shepherded by the United States on the treatment of waste water in small communities and a British-led study on waste-water facilities in the United Kingdom. Norway is carrying out a comparative study of water laws and institutions in the region. The World Bank has also carried out, under the auspices of the group, a survey of water conservation in the West Bank, Gaza and Jordan. At the last plenary meeting in Amman two new projects were approved by the group. The first, shepherded by the Netherlands, will focus on the potential of building a dam in the Nahal

Besor/Wadi Aza in order to enrich the aquifers in Gaza. The second, which will be led by Sweden, will focus on patterns of domestic water consumption and on ways of increasing public awareness of the need to control domestic consumption.

Enhancing water supply

Although conservation and improved management practices are important, it is equally necessary to find ways of increasing the supply and developing new sources of water for the region. Central to the working group's activities in this sphere is a German-led study, carried out in conjunction with the core regional parties, on the present and projected level of supply and demand for existing water resources among the core parties. The aim of the study is to arrive at mutually agreed assessments of the extent of their water needs in the future and of the likely gap between those needs and the supply of water from existing sources. The study will also critically evaluate the feasibility of the various solutions that have been proposed, ranging from desalination through pipelines to water importation, to meet the expected water needs of the region.

The working group has been especially active in exploring the potential benefits of desalination projects for the Middle East. Oman, in particular, has been a driving force in promoting activities in this sphere. As a first step, and in collaboration with a wide range of regional and non-regional experts, it produced a Worldwide Desalination Research and Technology Survey. At the plenary meeting in Muscat in April 1994, the working group endorsed Oman's proposal to set up a Middle East Desalination Research Centre to be based in Muscat. The aim of the centre will be to develop technically feasible and economically viable methods of desalination, thereby making desalinated water a more cost-effective option for states in the Middle East. The centre will also be active in providing a regional focus and in training personnel from the region who are currently working, or will work in the future, on desalination-related activities. This project has received widespread backing from the working group, and the United States and Oman have each committed $3 million to the centre. In September and December 1995 representatives from Oman, Israel, Japan, the United States and the European Union met to develop a detailed action plan to mobilize further resources for the centre and to develop its research programme.

A number of other activities have been agreed upon in this field. Japan is conducting a feasibility study for a brackish water desalination plant in Jordan, while the European Union is undertaking a similar project in Gaza. The working group has agreed to a Canadian proposal for the installation of rainwater catchment systems in Gaza. Canada has also produced a literature review on water technologies and Australia hosted a workshop in April–May 1995 on rainfall enhancement.

Concepts of regional cooperation and management

The working group has adopted a comprehensive plan for the training of professional water personnel in the region. By June 1995, eight of the fourteen training courses identified by this programme had been completed. The United Nations also organized a seminar in Geneva in December 1993 which assessed the various models for regional cooperation and management, while the United States hosted a workshop in April 1994 on weather forecasting.

All the proposals under consideration within the working group are based on the assumption of a high degree of cooperation among the regional parties. In order to manage their water resources more efficiently, it will be necessary for them to develop forms of regional cooperation and management structure. To this end, Jordan proposed at the meeting in Beijing that the working group should initiate discussions towards the formulation of a 'Water Charter' for the Middle East which would define the principles for regional cooperation and would serve as a mechanism for resolving differences on this subject. So far there has been little support for such a charter. However, the working group has taken the first steps in drawing up a set of guidelines and principles as proposed by the Steering Group.

5 THE WORKING GROUP ON THE ENVIRONMENT

In recent years, threats to, and the need to protect, the quality of the environment have moved from a rather lowly position on the international agenda to the forefront of world politics. The transborder nature of environmental issues has resulted in a redefinition of political space and requires the collaboration and cooperation of states. In response, the international community has created a number of arrangements and institutions and a new body of international law to manage these shared problems. At the national level, environment agencies have been set up, environmental legislation has been passed and the public has been made aware of the need for environmental protection. These efforts have been forward-looking and extensive and have recognized the multiple interdependencies involved in these issues.

The creation of a Working Group on the Environment as part of the Middle East peace process is a reflection of this growing international concern and a recognition that multilateral cooperation is essential if any headway is to be made on the plethora of environmental problems facing the Middle East. Japan has taken on the responsibility for this group as the gavel-holder, with the European Union and the United States serving as co-organizers. The group has met seven times, most recently in a 'clustered' meeting with the Working Group on Water Resources in Amman in June 1995. (For other dates and locations see Appendix 2.)

The shared perception of the need for collective action has enabled these talks to proceed in a positive and constructive atmosphere. On the second day of the 1993 meetings in Tokyo and Cairo the parties convened in a series of smaller groups to discuss specific areas of cooperation in greater depth. These informal sessions were led by the EU on the management of the east Mediterranean coastal area; by Italy on solid waste management; by Japan on producing an environmental code of conduct; by the United States on waste-water treatment for small communities; by the World Bank on desertification; and by Jordan on environmental education. These informal sessions, a configuration which has also been adopted by the water working group, have proved to be a great success. In the meetings in The Hague, Manama and Amman further sessions have been held to discuss the Upper Gulf of Aqaba oil spill contingency project, environmental impact assessment, environmental health and pesticides, a Middle East 'year of the environment', regional environmental centres and the environmental profile of Gaza.

While the notion of collective goods has been prominent in these talks, there have been two areas of friction between Israel and the Arabs. The first concerned the demand by the Palestinians during the first three rounds for the setting up of a Palestinian agency for the protection of the environment. Although Israel was prepared to acknowledge the need for training programmes in the occupied territories, it was not prepared to accept the creation via the multilaterals of an agency which would be regarded by the Palestinians as a national authority. A clumsily worded compromise was found whereby the working group noted the growing need for 'more effective and structured implementation of institutions and capacity building efforts by the regional parties including the West Bank and Gaza'. The issue ceased to be a bone of contention with the signing of the Declaration of Principles which calls for the establishment of a Palestinian Environmental Authority (Article VII).

The second area of controversy has centred on the desire of the Arab states, led by Egypt, to include radioactive waste and pollution on the agenda. Much to the consternation of Israel, which is unwilling to discuss nuclear issues in any form, this issue was raised at the meeting in Cairo. In the absence of any consensus and in light of unyielding Israeli opposition, no reference was made to this subject in the concluding remarks of the gavel–holder. This caused considerable disquiet among the Arab states, resulting in the final session overrunning by three hours as they attempted, ultimately without success, to amend the closing state-ment of the meeting.[1] This issue continued to plague the next meeting in The Hague, where again no consensus was reached. This time, however, the sharp differences between Israel and Egypt over the issue were noted in the concluding remarks by the gavel-holder. It was also agreed, in spite of Israel's objection, that in order to facilitate discussion of this issue in future meetings, the participants should be encouraged to submit their relevant laws, guidelines, rules and procedures to the gavel-holder in advance.

This issue was finally laid to rest shortly before the opening of the sixth round of talks following a compromise reached between Israel's Minister of the Environment Yossi Sarid, who headed Israel's delegation to the meeting in Manama, and the Egyptian Foreign Minister Amr Moussa.[2] Under the agreement reached the issue of hazardous wastes, including a discussion of the environmental effects of low-level radioactive waste as well as of chemical and toxic waste, would now be included as a separate item on the agenda. These issues would be discussed in separate inter-sessional meetings of experts from the region. The first meeting on national rules and regulations on low-level radioactive waste was held in Washington in May 1995. A second meeting on chemical and toxic wastes, hosted by Switzerland, was planned for early 1996.

The remaining agenda items of the environment talks cover four main areas: maritime pollution; environmental management; water quality, sewage and waste management; and desertification.

Maritime pollution

Since the opening round of the environment working group in Tokyo in 1992 there has been a recognition by all the states along the coastal line of the Gulf of Aqaba of the need for regional organization and coordination in order to prevent water pollution resulting from accidents at sea, and also of the need for the capability to deal rapidly and efficiently with such pollution when it does occur. At the plenary meeting in Cairo in 1993, the World Bank also reported on an environment action plan based on its study of the Gulf of Aqaba.[3] At the same meeting there was strong consensual support for an Egyptian proposal for the establishment of a regional centre to coordinate preparedness for marine disasters and emergencies. As a first step Israel, Jordan and Egypt have drawn up a joint plan for dealing with oil spills in the Gulf of Aqaba. This programme, the Upper Gulf of Aqaba oil spill contingency project, involves the setting up of emergency response facilities in the northern half of the Gulf of Aqaba in Nuweibah and Aqaba, and the upgrading of the existing facility in Eilat. These three centres will be linked by a communications network, and teams from Israel, Jordan and Egypt will participate in joint training sessions. The European Union is financing equipment for the Nuweibah centre and Japan is funding the Aqaba centre, while Israel is upgrading the facilities in Eilat. In support of this project the United States, working alongside Jordanian and Israeli experts, has produced environmental sensitivity maps of the Gulf of Aqaba for the Jordanian and Israeli coastlines and is currently completing a similar map for the Egyptian coastline. The regional parties have also called for similar initiatives to be developed to combat potential chemical and ballast pollution in the Gulf.

A number of other inter-sessional activities have taken place in this field. In June 1993 Japan conducted a seminar on maritime disaster prevention and in February of that year the United States hosted a workshop on hazardous material accidents, while the European Union has produced a report for the integrated management of the eastern Mediterranean coastal area.

Environmental management

The most significant achievement of the environment working group so far has been the adoption, during the sixth round of talks, of the 'Bahrain Environmental Code of Conduct for the Middle East' (see Appendix 3). Under the stewardship of Japan, the Cairo Consultative Group, consisting of nearly twenty delegations, met in Egypt in February and July 1994 to draw up this document. The code of conduct establishes a common set of principles and guidelines which should govern the developmental policies of each of the regional parties. Although the code does not commit the parties to any formal legal obligations, it does define the future direction of environmental programmes and legislation, identify the major environmental issues facing the region and list a set of joint actions to meet those challenges. The parties recognize the interdependence of their environmental policies and the need to 'coordinate their environ-mental policies with one another and cooperate in protecting the overall environment in the region in good faith and in a spirit of partnership'. To achieve this goal, they have resolved to 'cooperate in promoting appropriate technology and capability to tackle environmental issues by joint projects, joint research and other activities where appropriate; facilitate the transfer of technology, know-how, and information; notify one another of environmental situations that have regional or transboundary impacts'.[4]

Another important area of activity identified by the working group is increasing awareness and knowledge of the environmental issues affecting the region. The group has approved proposals by Jordan and Bahrain respectively for the establishment of a regional environmental resource and training centre in Amman, and a centre on environmental information and technology transfer in Manama. In April 1995 an inter-sessional gathering of experts met in Manama and an ad hoc committee has been formed to discuss issues related to the setting-up of the Bahraini centre.

Other projects and inter-sessional activities in this sphere have included a workshop organized by the United States in Cairo in March 1994 on environmental monitoring and measurement; a project also led by the United States on the environmental health effects of pesticides, with two workshops on this issue in Egypt and Jordan; and a project shepherded by Austria focusing on the monitoring of air quality in the eastern Mediterranean.

Canada has been active in the field of environmental impact assessment. The working group has supported a Canadian proposal to create an environmental impact assessment forum to promote the exchange of information among the regional parties. As part of its efforts in this area it organized, in conjunction with the water resources working group, a training course for senior administrators and practitioners on this subject, held in Cairo in November 1994.

The Netherlands has been working with the Palestinians on a joint project to develop an environmental profile for the Gaza Strip. The Palestinians, with the support of Jordan and Egypt, have proposed that the working group should also initiate a similar environmental profile for the Jordan rift valley.

Water quality, sewage and waste management

A number of workshops have been held in this field. Japan organized a workshop on industrial pollution control technologies at the end of January 1994, and Italy hosted a seminar on solid waste management in June 1994. In conjunction with the water resources working group, the United States has been leading a project on waste-water treatment for small communities. The planning phase for this project has been completed and efforts are now being directed towards securing funding for the construction of a waste-water and reuse facility in the West Bank village of Taffouh to serve the needs of the local inhabitants.

Desertification

The battle against desertification and the control of natural resource degradation has been adopted as one of the priority areas for the work of the environment group. The World Bank has assumed a leading role in this area and, with the cooperation of Israel, Jordan, Egypt, Tunisia and the Palestinians, has prepared an operational plan which was adopted by the fifth round of meetings in The Hague. This plan, the 'Initiative for Collaboration to Control Natural Resource Degradation of Arid Lands in the Middle East', calls for the establishment of five regional centres, each dealing with a specific area of activity. Egypt will coordinate work on the adaptation of vegetation to desert conditions, Tunisia will focus on the use of brackish and waste water for irrigation, Israel will be responsible for forestation, and the issue of livestock and grazing will be coordinated by Jordan. The project also calls for the establishment of a Palestinian Institute for Arid Lands Research which will deal with professional training in these areas.

6 THE WORKING GROUP ON REFUGEES

The decision to establish a working group on refugees was made shortly before the organizational meeting in Moscow at the behest of the Palestinians. The gavel-holder for the group is Canada, with the United States, the European Union and Japan acting as co-organizers. It has met seven times (for details see Appendix 2).

The inclusion within the framework of the multilateral talks of a working group focusing on the needs of the Palestinian refugees appears, at first glance, to be puzzling.[1] Given the political nature of this issue, a solution to the refugee problem can be found only through bilateral negotiations, either in direct discussions between the regional parties or in trilateral or quadripartite mechanisms established in various agreements. Indeed, Article V of the Declaration of Principles states explicitly that the refugee question will be discussed in the permanent status negotiations between Israel and the Palestinians. Article XII also calls for the setting-up of a joint Israeli–Palestinian–Jordanian–Egyptian committee which will decide upon 'the modalities for the admission of persons displaced from the West Bank and Gaza Strip in 1967'. At the same time, many of the issues surrounding this question cannot be resolved exclusively at the bilateral level. Even though the future of the Palestinian refugees can only be decided through direct negotiations between Israel and the PLO, the outcome of any agreements reached will touch upon the interests of many other parties in the region and therefore warrant consideration in a multilateral framework.

Questions relating to the future status, welfare and living conditions of the Palestinian refugees are technical and complex, and do not lend themselves to quick answers. If there is to be a resolution to the Palestinian refugee problem, which lies at the very heart of the Arab–Israeli conflict and the peace process, the parties will have to talk openly and freely about

29

a range of highly charged and sensitive issues. Such efforts will require the active participation of the international community, extending beyond mere diplomatic encouragement to include the provision of significant financial resources in support of a final settlement.

Not surprisingly, given the sensitivity of this issue and the widely divergent starting points of Israel and the Palestinians, the functioning of this working group was fraught with difficulties during the opening rounds. The Palestinians saw the group as a forum for addressing the substantive concerns and the political rights of the refugees; Israel, on the other hand, regarded discussion of humanitarian aspects and of improvements in the welfare of the refugees solely as a confidence-building measure and not as a substantive issue. Controversy, during the opening two rounds in particular, revolved around two issues: the participation in these talks of Palestinians from outside the occupied territories; and the inclusion of family reunification as an item on the agenda, since this is an issue which is central to the question of the refugees *per se* and not a matter of their general welfare. Israel has regarded this item with deep suspicion and has viewed it as a potential back door for the discussion of a Palestinian 'right to return'.[2] For the Palestinians, progress on this issue is both a substantive matter and an important confidence-building measure.

The first two rounds of talks in Ottawa were dominated by a procedural dispute centring on the composition of the Palestinian delegation. Israel boycotted the first meeting in protest at the presence in the delegation of Palestinians from outside the occupied territories, a move which they saw as directly contravening the terms of the Madrid conference.[3] Under a compromise agreement brokered by Egypt's Foreign Minister Amr Moussa at the beginning of October 1992, the new Labour government in Israel agreed to the participation of Palestinians from the diaspora provided that they were not members of the PLO or Palestine National Council and that the issue of the 'right to return' was not raised. To the consternation of the Israelis, the Palestinian delegation for the second round was headed by Dr Muhammad Hallaj, a long-standing member of the PNC. This caused the Israelis to boycott the proceedings again. After a day of intense negotiations on the sidelines, the fortuitous discovery that Hallaj's membership of the PNC had lapsed in 1991 brought this procedural impasse to an end. The delay, however, left only half a day for discussion.

The broad mandate of the refugee working group is to alleviate the plight and suffering of peoples displaced by the Arab–Israeli conflict. Its work is predicated on the assumption that improving the living conditions of the Palestinian refugees and the search for a political solution are complementary rather than mutually exclusive activities, and that any achievements in ameliorating the daily existence of the Palestinian refugees should not be prejudicial to determining their final status and the political settlement of this question.

Since its inception the refugee working group has been active in three broad areas: defining the scope of the refugee problem, encouraging a dialogue on the issues involved and mobilizing the resources required to address them. During its first two meetings the group identified six themes and allocated shepherds to be responsible for work in these areas. These six themes, which have formed the basis of the inter-sessional activities of the refugee group, are: databases (Norway); family reunification (France); human resources development, job creation and vocational training (United States); public health (Italy), child welfare (Sweden); and economic and social infrastructure (European Union).

Defining the scope of the refugee problem

For the refugee problem to be effectively addressed, there has to be a common understanding of its scope and nature. Under the stewardship of Norway, as shepherd for the database theme, the refugee working group has sponsored efforts to expand and update existing databases on refugees and establish well-organized, accessible and objective data on the refugee community. The provision of reliable data on the Palestinian population is essential for the efficient planning and coordination of policy-related studies, for determining priorities for future activities and for assessing the impact of alternative political choices.

The Institute for Applied Social Science in Oslo (FAFO) has played a leading role in this area. During the third round of talks the working group received a report on the findings of its survey, undertaken in July 1992, on living conditions in the occupied territories. This was followed at the end of September 1993 by a seminar of experts held in Oslo in order to analyse the findings of the study and to submit a series of recommendations. As conditions in the occupied territories were changing rapidly, the FAFO carried out a second survey in November 1993 and presented its findings to the plenary meeting in Cairo. The working group has also underlined the need for data on the living conditions of Palestinian refugees elsewhere in the region, especially in Jordan, Syria and Lebanon, and FAFO is currently conducting a survey of living conditions in Jordan, which will include a specific refugee component. FAFO is also producing an inventory of recent research on Palestinian refugees and is undertaking a project on living conditions in the refugee camps.

The working group has provided logistical support to the newly established Palestinian Central Bureau of Statistics (PCBS) and to the bureau's work, in cooperation with FAFO, on a demographic survey of the West Bank and Gaza. The group has also encouraged states to offer financial support for two proposals developed by the United Nations Relief and Works Agency (UNRWA) – presented to the meeting at Antalya – for a unified registration scheme for Palestinian refugees and for a project to reorganize and safely store its archives.

The efforts of the working group to define the scope of the refugee problem have not been confined exclusively to the database theme. Italy, as shepherd for public health, and Sweden, as shepherd for child welfare, have undertaken missions to the region to assess needs and possible projects in these spheres. The European Union has also completed an inventory of continuing efforts to assist Palestinian refugees and presented a report of its findings to the Antalya meeting.

Encouraging a dialogue

The second major area of the group's work is the encouragement of a dialogue on the issues involved. A fundamental element in promoting this dialogue is the work undertaken by France on the question of family reunification. Aside from the initial problem of representation at the table, this issue has proved to be the most difficult to address and the main point of contention between Israel and the Palestinians. In order to bridge the gap between the sides, the French diplomat Bernard Bajolet visited the Middle East at the end of April 1993 to clarify the views of Egypt, Jordan, Israel and the Palestinians on this subject. Following his preliminary report to the third round in Oslo, the working group issued Bajolet with a mandate to make a second visit to the region and to submit a set of proposals to the plenary meeting in Tunis. After this second visit, Bajolet outlined a number of recommendations, including:

- an increase in the number of beneficiaries of family reunification;
- improvement of and greater transparency in Israeli procedures;
- measures to facilitate reunification;
- measures to widen the field of applications for family reunification;
- measures to prevent the appearance of new cases of family separation.

Several of Bajolet's proposals have already been accepted by Israel. At a press conference after the Tunis meeting, Yossi Beilin, then Israel's Deputy Foreign Minister, announced that Israel had agreed to process 2,000 cases each year, a fourfold increase on the previous annual quota, in a move designed to benefit 5,000 Palestinians.[4] Israel has indicated that it would be willing to make available texts governing its procedures and its criteria for family reunification. In the future family reunification will apply systematically to spouses, children under the age of sixteen and serious humanitarian cases. Israel also informed Bajolet that it would reduce significantly the time taken to process applications from an average of one year to a maximum of three months.

The working group accepted Bajolet's recommendation that an inter-sessional sub-working group, composed of jurists and relevant experts, be established in order to define the concept of the family within the Middle East and thereby assist in determining the criteria for family reunification. This group met in Tunis in February 1994 and reported on its findings to the Antalya meeting at the end of the year. France also convened a seminar in Paris in November 1994 to review the situation regarding family reunification and to assess the changes to procedures and practices bought about by the implementation of the 4 May 1995 Gaza–Jericho accord and the Israel–Jordan peace treaty.

The achievements on the question of family reunification should not be overstated. They fall far short of the expectations and aspirations of the Palestinians. While some progress has been made in a number of areas, including the establishment of certain principles and criteria for the reunification of families and increases in quotas, no significant new measures have been adopted since the meeting in Tunis in October 1993. Nor, however, should the modest achievements be hastily dismissed. The success of the assiduous efforts of the French in this sphere reflects the benefits of 'fractionation' – breaking down problem areas into their constituent parts – and the value of third-party mediation.[5] This piece-meal approach not only offers the parties a greater familiarity with the subject matter but also provides them with a gradually increasing competence and confidence in the negotiating process.

Mobilizing resources

A substantive part of the working group's efforts has been concerned with improving the daily lives of the Palestinian refugees and with mobilizing the necessary financial resources to serve that purpose. These activities have been undertaken with the explicit acknowledgment that attending to the immediate welfare of the refugee population should not prejudice their political rights or future status in any final settlement reached between Israel and the Palestinians. These efforts have focused on the four themes identified in the early deliberations of the working group: human resources development, job creation and vocational training; public health; child welfare; and economic and social infrastructure. Many of these issues overlap directly with the activities of the regional economic development working group (the United States is shepherd for training programmes, and Italy for health, in both groups). A large percentage of the funds mobilized by the refugee working group has been channelled through UNRWA, with particular emphasis on its Peace Implementation Programme (PIP) which has already received commitments of over $100 million to improve the living conditions of the Palestinian refugees.

The refugee working group has provided support for emergency housing in Lebanon; health clinics, vocational training centres and emergency housing in Syria; and secondary schools, maternal and child healthcare, and vocational training centres in Jordan. It has also provided fundamental funding for the training of Palestinian refugees in areas ranging from public health and nursing through construction trades to agricultural skills and public administration. The group has also attended to the health needs of the Palestinians by providing supplies and equipment for UNWRA and Palestinian Red Crescent Society clinics and has provided help in setting up a central public health laboratory for the West Bank and Gaza. Italy, as shepherd for health, has run a seminar on the overall health needs of the refugees and has also organized a workshop on Palestinian nursing. Finally, the working group, through the work of Sweden as shepherd, has been involved in the planning and implementation of a programme developed by UNICEF which concentrates on the needs of Palestinian children.

Recent meetings of the refugee working group have begun to resemble donor pledging conferences on behalf of the Palestinian refugees. The shepherds in the group have used the occasion to report on their past activities and to announce new projects initiated by themselves or by other donors, and have encouraged others to join them in their endeavours. So far, the meetings have largely skirted around the highly charged political issues which lie at the heart of the refugee question. The value and importance of the refugee working group lies in less grandiose achievements. It is the sole forum within the framework of the current peace process where the interests of the Palestinan population outside Gaza and the West Bank have been voiced. At a time when nearly all bilateral aid to the Palestinians has been channelled to the Palestinian National Authority in Gaza and the West Bank, it is vital that the international community should not forsake the needs and concerns of the refugee population. No just and lasting settlement to the Arab–Israel conflict can be found without addressing comprehensively the political, civil, economic and social rights of the Palestinian refugees. That is, and remains, the challenge facing the refugee working group.

7 THE WORKING GROUP ON ARMS CONTROL AND REGIONAL SECURITY

The idea of arms control is not foreign to the Arab–Israeli conflict. Throughout the history of the conflict, Egypt, Syria, Jordan and Israel have agreed to a variety of arms control and confidence-building measures in respect of the disengagement of their forces, demilitarization, limitation of forces agreements and military-to-military contacts in mixed armistice commissions. These measures, however, have been limited and modest in scope and have been applied in specific contexts, usually in the aftermath of hostilities between the sides. Yet, such arms control arrangements did play an integral part in developing the peace process between Egypt and Israel, and a number of specific provisions were incorporated to underwrite the Egypt–Israel peace treaty. Similarly, the Jordan–Israel peace treaty incorporates a number of arms control measures which address the security concerns of each side.

Until recently, however, the idea of exploring arms control possibilities in a broader context, as a mechanism for advancing regional security across the whole Middle East, was dismissed as being, at best, foolhardy and irrelevant. The mindsets of the various governments have not been considered conducive to support for concepts such as mutual, collective or cooperative security. National security has been perceived as a zero-sum game, wherein gains for one side have been seen as constituting a potential threat to the other. States have pursued their national security interests primarily through the expansion and modernization of their military forces. There has been little recognition that arms control or arms reductions and the search for political agreements in this area would serve either national or mutual interests. Instead, arms control has been seen as a device to constrain the military capabilities of states and has therefore been regarded as potentially undermining rather than enhancing their security needs.[1]

The geostrategic and geopolitical realities of the region have also been regarded as antithetical to arms control. The Middle East is characterized by numerous long-standing and bitter historical rivalries. Unlike the situation in Europe during the Cold War, when a clear and defined military stand-off existed between the two blocs, NATO and the Warsaw Pact, in the Middle East most states face multiple threats to their security from their neighbours. No single, central balance of power exists in the region: instead, there are a number of overlapping balances of power at work. Consequently, states have been locked into a web of mutually reinforcing conflicts. Potential political and military developments in each of these conflicts feed directly into the strategic calculations of all parties in the region. There are disparities in the force levels and structures of the armies of the region and massive assymetries in the quantity and quality of weaponry possessed by states. Nor are the geographical and political parameters of the region clearly defined. The actions of states located even at the periphery of the region, such as Turkey and Pakistan, have repercussions for all actors in the Middle East.[2] These factors have made the potential application of arms control measures to the Middle East in the past neither feasible nor desirable. At the same time, however, they also serve to underline the pressing need to address security concerns in a regional context and not solely on a bilateral basis.

The Working Group on Arms Control and Regional Security (ACRS) marks the official launching, for the first time in the history of the Middle East, of a regional arms control process. With the co-sponsors of the peace process, the United States and Russia, as the gavel holders, this working group has held six rounds of talks (see Appendix 2 for details). Unlike the other working groups, the attendance of states from outside the region at these meetings has been restricted. Originally, Israel wanted only the two co-sponsors and the regional parties to participate. After the first round, the membership was expanded to include Australia, Canada, China, India, Japan, Turkey, Ukraine, a representative from the European Union and a representative from the EFTA countries. It was not until the third round, held in Washington in May 1993, that Israel agreed to the participation of the Palestinians and a delegation from the United

Nations. The question of whether to permit all the member states of the European Union to participate, in their own right, in this working group was not resolved until the fourth round in Qatar.

Not surprisingly, given the sharp differences in their threat perceptions and security concerns, the proposals and concepts presented by Israel and the Arab states have differed significantly, especially with respect to the question of nuclear weapons. The Arab states, led by Egypt, have focused on the need to address the problem of weapons of mass destruction in the region and have sought to place the question of Israel's nuclear capability on the agenda. While accepting the need for confidence-building mechanisms, the Arab states have argued forcefully that the discussion of this issue should not be ignored and have indeed defined it as an important confidence-building measure in itself.[3] Israel has turned a deaf ear to this argument. The Israeli approach is diametrically opposite to the Arab position and has centred on the necessity of developing a set of confidence-building measures such as the prior notification of large-scale military exercises and the development of hot-lines, crisis prevention mechanisms and verification procedures. Restraints on strategic systems and the issue of nuclear weapons are seen as belonging to the last stage in the process.[4]

The position of the United States, which has orchestrated these talks, has to a large extent mirrored the Israeli approach. In his opening address to the organizational meeting in Moscow in January 1992, US Secretary of State Baker stressed the need for an incremental approach to arms control, with some initial modest confidence-building measures.

> In the first instance, we envision offering the regional parties our thinking about potential approaches to arms control, drawing on a vast reservoir of experience stemming from attempts to regulate military competition in Europe and other regions. From this base, the group might move forward to considering a set of modest confidence building or transparency measures covering notifications of selected military-related activities and crisis prevention communications. The purpose would be to lessen the prospects for incidents and miscalculation that could lead to heightened competition or even conflict.[5]

The assessment of the United States is that the political conditions within the Middle East are not yet ripe, and that the bilateral Arab–Israeli talks have not advanced sufficiently, for securing the cooperation of the states in serious efforts to control the spread of conventional and non-conventional weapons in the region. On the contrary, it has argued, to raise issues at such an early stage in the process would be damaging and counterproductive. Accordingly it has refrained, so far, from introducing the May 1991 Bush arms control initiative for the Middle East for discussion in these talks.

Inter-sessional activities and projects

The first two rounds of talks, held in May and September 1992, were conducted in seminar form and were designed to familiarize the participants with the general issues and background to arms control and confidence-building measures, particularly in respect of the US–Soviet and European experiences. During these meetings the parties from the region were encouraged to air their general views on regional security and to explore avenues for potential cooperation. Not surprisingly, the discussions, both formal and informal, displayed wide gaps between the parties' evaluations of one another's military capabilities and threat perceptions.

During the third round of talks in May 1993 consensus was reached on the need to expand the scope of the working group, to increase the frequency of contacts between the plenary sessions and to initiate a more focused set of activities. To this end, a programme of inter-sessional activities was drawn up. These consisted of joint visits to an airbase in the United Kingdom and a military communications facility in The Hague, and the observation of a NATO military exercise in Denmark. The parties also agreed to hold a number of workshops: on verification mechanisms (held in Cairo); on communication measures (with the Netherlands as shepherd); on the exchange of military information and the prior notification of military exercises (with Turkey as shepherd); on long-term arms control objectives and declaratory measures (with the United States and Russia as shepherds); and on maritime measures (with Canada as shepherd). Other activities, which would be coordinated by the United

States and Russia, included the compilation and analysis of arms control proposals for the Middle East; analysis of the various confidence-building measures associated with arms control; assessment of the geographical scope of plans for arms control and regional security measures in the Middle East; and the possibility of a centre for conflict prevention in the region.

The fourth round of talks, held in November 1993, reviewed the inter-sessional activities which had taken place since the previous plenary session and drew up a programme of further activities. It also decided to cluster its work into two separate tracks: an operational 'basket', concentrating on short-term security and confidence-building measures; and a conceptual 'basket', focusing on the longer-term security issues facing the Middle East and the overall aims and objectives of the arms control process.

The 'operational basket'

There have been three sessions to consider the operational basket (see Appendix 2). The activities have centred on developing practical steps for advancing cooperation on maritime issues, communications and the exchange of military information.

Maritime issues

Canada has acted as shepherd in facilitating work among the regional parties on developing a number of maritime confidence-building measures. In particular, the drafting of two documents for approval at the next ACRS plenary meeting has been completed: the first aimed at reducing the risk of naval accidents by preventing incidents at sea (INCSEA), and the second on maritime search and rescue operations (SAR). In order to promote a greater level of cooperation and understanding of the issues involved in these areas, Canada has hosted a meeting of senior naval officers from the region. The regional parties have also agreed to participate jointly in the observation of a INCSEA and SAR exercise. Originally, it was intended that this demonstration would be held off the Tunisian coast during the spring of 1995. Negative advance publicity about this operation, however, including scepticism about Tunisia's capacity to mount the exercise, led to its postponement, though the Tunisian government has since reiterated its willingness to host such an event in the future.

Communications

The Netherlands, as shepherd for this area, has played an important role in helping set up an ACRS communication network. This network became operational in March 1995, for the time being using the communications infrastructure of the OSCE centre in The Hague as a hub. End-user stations have become operational in Tel Aviv and Cairo and others will shortly be installed in the region. Regional experts are also in the final stages of preparing the technical specifications for a permanent hub for the network, which will be located in Cairo.

Exchange of military information

Turkey has played an important role in promoting cooperation in this area. Specifically, the regional parties have drawn up four draft agreements for presentation to the next ACRS plenary. These cover the prior notification of certain military exercises; the exchange of the curriculum vitae of senior military officers; the exchange of unclassified military publications and educational and training manuals; and voluntary invitations to visit defence installations. In respect of the last of these, Israel has extended an open invitation to all participants in the ACRS talks to visit one of its military installations.

The 'conceptual basket'

The conceptual basket has also been the subject of three sessions (see Appendix 2). The aim of this basket is to provide a framework for the drafting of a set of principles which will govern the nature of future security relations among the states of the Middle East and lay down the basis upon which future negotiations in the ACRS talks will proceed. The conceptual basket has also focused on developing ideas for new institutions and mechanisms to provide for security and cooperation in the Middle East.

A regional security centre

From the start of the multilaterals, Jordan has consistently advocated the need for a new regional institutional framework to support the objectives and reinforce the activities of arms control talks.[6] After a series of intensive discussions throughout 1994, the plenary meeting in Tunis endorsed the idea of setting up a regional security centre. The headquarters of this centre, once established, will be located in Amman, with related facilities in Doha and Tunis. A meeting was held in Amman in September 1995 to finalize the mandate for this centre and to sketch out its initial tasks. It is envisaged that the centre will serve as a venue for seminars and training on arms control and regional security and that it will host activities aimed at implementing any specific measures approved by future ACRS plenaries, such as the exchange of military information, the avoiding of incidents at sea and the prior notification of certain military activities. The Amman centre, together with the sites in Doha and Tunis, will be linked to the ACRS communication network; and the software for a Middle East arms control data bank, currently being developed by the Russians, would be installed in all three centres. The role of this centre is expected to evolve over time to include specific tasks traditionally associated with crisis prevention, conflict management and conflict resolution.

Declaration of Principles

The first meeting of the ACRS 'conceptual basket' was devoted to the drawing up of a 'Declaration of Principles on Arms Control and Regional Security'. After four days of intensive discussions, the parties finalized a draft text consisting of three parts: a set of principles governing future security relations among states in the region; a set of guidelines to direct the arms control process; and a statement of the long-term aims of the ACRS talks.[7] It was widely anticipated that this draft would be endorsed by the next plenary meeting three months later; however, these hopes were dashed during that meeting when several of the Arab delegations, led most vociferously by Saudi Arabia, objected to many of the clauses dealing with the political nature of relations among all the states of the region.[8] It was then hoped that the parties would convene in Vienna at the beginning of the following month for a special inter-sessional meeting aimed at ironing out these differences and finalizing the text. Again the Saudi delegation objected, arguing that such a meeting would be premature, and it was not until a further three months had passed that discussions about the Declaration of Principles were resumed, in Paris in mid-October. Although there was some meeting of minds in Paris, the parties did not succeed in reconciling their differences. In particular, a sharp division emerged during that meeting, and at the subsequent ACRS plenary in Tunis, between Israel and Egypt over the inclusion of a common statement on weapons of mass destruction.

This issue beleaguered discussions on the Declaration of Principles throughout 1995 and, despite the best efforts of the Americans to find a formula acceptable to both sides, little progress was achieved in bridging the divide. The dispute over the nuclear question rapidly developed into a public souring of relations between Israel and Egypt in the months prior to the UN conference on the renewal of the Nuclear Non-Proliferation Treaty (NPT) in April. Exchanges between the two sides became increasingly heated and acrimonious, with Egypt threatening to withhold its support for an indefinite extension to the non-proliferation treaty unless Israel became a signatory to the NPT and and was prepared to open up its nuclear facilities to international inspection.[9]

The dispute continued to plague relations between the two countries even after the conclusion of the NPT renewal conference. There were signs, however, towards the end of the year that both Egypt and Israel were eager to put their differences behind them. During Shimon Peres' first visit to Egypt as Israel's new Prime Minister in December, President Mubarak announced that Egypt would desist from pressurizing Israel to join the NPT until a settlement with Syria had been reached.[10] Before leaving for Cairo, Peres had publicly hinted that in the context of a regional peace agreement with all the Arab states Israel would be prepared to forgo its nuclear deterrent.[11]

In the meantime, given the successful renewal of the NPT treaty in the middle of May there was widespread expectation that the ACRS working group would be able to resume and finalize the Declaration of Principles. These hopes proved to be short-lived and the nuclear issue continued to bedevil the deliberations of the working group. In the third meeting on the conceptual basket, held in Helsinki a fortnight after the winding-up of the NPT review conference, Egypt re-emphasized its concerns and its resolve that the ACRS working group should not ignore this issue. It became apparent during that meeting that Egypt's dissatisfaction extended beyond Israel's refusal to address the issue of weapons of mass destruction and that it had become increasingly disillusioned with the pace and direction of the working group, which after three years of talks had yet to produce any tangible outcomes. It had not initiated any substantive negotiations on arms control, nor even agreed on the elements for beginning such negotiations. Many of the issues under discussion within the ACRS group had only the most tenuous links with actual arms control. To move the process forward, Egypt called for the convening of a group of experts to examine ways of embarking on concrete negotiations in the working group. Egypt's disenchantment with the lack of specific achievements and the overall focus of ACRS led to the postponement of the plenary meeting originally scheduled for September.[12]

The modest progress of the arms control and regional security working group has been limited by the absence of key regional actors. Syria and Lebanon have boycotted all the sessions of these talks. Equally important, Iraq, Iran and Libya have not been invited to participate in these meetings and will need to be drawn into the process at some point in the future. The absence of these states underscores the embryonic nature of this process and the limited outcomes that it can be expected to produce at this early stage. Yet even though the very limited progress made and the substantive issues under discussion have left some participants dissatisfied, the group's overall contribution should not be written off. Though the parties have failed, so far, to put their signatures to a Declaration of Principles on arms control and regional security in the Middle East, considerable areas of common ground have been found in the drafting of this text. Likewise, the agreement to establish a regional security centre and a telecommunications network represents a shared recognition of the importance of developing institutional frameworks and new mechanisms in order to reinforce future cooperative security arrangements in the Middle East. The existence of the ACRS working group, which itself represents an important confidence-building measure, is a significant first step in facilitating communication among the parties, in shifting long-held, ingrained attitudes and in developing a new common strategic culture in the Middle East.

8 THE WORKING GROUP ON REGIONAL ECONOMIC DEVELOPMENT

The working group on regional economic development (REDWG) is the largest of the five groups, both in terms of the number of participants and in terms of the number of projects and inter-sessional activities. The European Union acts as 'gavel-holder' for this group, with the United States and Japan serving as co-organizers. It has met six times (see Appendix 2); the seventh round of talks is scheduled for the middle of March 1996, and will be held in Amman.

By its very nature this group has the widest scope for developing areas of future cooperation among states in the Middle East and the greatest potential for effecting real change in the living conditions of the peoples of the region. The purpose of this working group reflects most fully the long-term goal of the multilateral talks, namely the creation of a new set of mutually beneficial relations between the parties and the building of a new era of economic prosperity for the region as a whole. Peace will only be sustainable in the Middle East if bilateral agreements, once concluded, are accompanied by a long-term process of economic cooperation among all the parties of region. The underlying premise for this working group is to be found in the functionalist thesis that the rewards of economic cooperation will drive the search and strengthen the foundations for political agreements. By becoming enmeshed in an ever-widening web of economic, technical and welfare interdependences, states are forced to set aside their political and/or ideological differences. Regional economic cooperation can only be pursued successfully in the context of peace and one creates the impetus for the other. At the same time, the active engagement in the search for regional solutions to economic and social problems can in itself consolidate and strengthen the peace process. Equally, the development of such regional cooperation has been seen as a powerful tool for stimulating economic growth and social development, for helping reduce regional economic disparities and the level of conflict, and ultimately for making peace irreversible.

Effectively excluded from the bilateral negotiations and the arms control talks, the European Union has been active in promoting ideas and ventures for future economic cooperation among the parties of the region. During the first three rounds of these talks a list of ten spheres of activity was drawn up, and 'shepherds' were assigned to take responsibility for the running of projects in each of these areas. The majority of these projects focus either on infrastructural development or on exploring areas of sectoral coordination. The areas are: communications and transport (led by France); energy (EU); tourism (Japan); agriculture (Spain); financial markets (United Kingdom); trade (Germany); training (United States); networks (EU); institutions, sectors and principles (Egypt); and bibliography (Canada).

The fourth round of talks took place shortly after the signing of the Declaration of Principles between Israel and the Palestinians. In the light of the breakthrough at the bilateral level there was an overwhelming recognition in Copenhagen of the need to intensify the workings of the REDWG to ensure that its activities would not become marginalized. Accordingly the group adopted the Copenhagen Action Plan, which outlined thirty-three different ventures (see Appendix 4). This plan has subsequently formed the working basis of the activities of the REDWG. At the plenary meetings in Rabat and Bonn, the shepherds have reported on the various activities undertaken and have announced new initiatives within their respective spheres of the Copenhagen Action Plan. In order to finance these activities, the European Union announced at the meeting in Rome that it would allocate $6 million for the preparation of feasibility studies and a further $9.2 million for the preparation of studies and the running of inter-sessional activities for the rapid implementation of the Copenhagen Action Plan.

Although the primary focus of the working group has been on fostering cooperation at the regional level, it has also been an important forum, especially during the early meetings, for addressing the economic needs of the Palestinians. At the Paris meeting in October 1992, in response to an initiative by the European Community, the World Bank was asked to produce a report on the economy of the occupied territories and to draw up a list of priority projects to overcome the infrastructural restraints to cooperation in the region. After a year of intensive consultations involving several field visits, the World Bank submitted its findings to the meeting in Copenhagen.[1] It is noteworthy that the report on the occupied territories, which forms the basis for directing $2.4 billion of the financial aid pledged to the Palestinians by the donors' conference held in Washington on 1 October 1992, was commissioned within the context of the multilateral talks and not the bilateral negotiations. The mechanism for directing this assistance to the Palestinians was a source of friction between the Europeans and the United States, which wanted the World Bank to have exclusive control of the aid plan. The unilateral calling of the donors' conference by the United States, combined with the desire of the Americans to remove the economic development of the occupied territories from the remit of the REDWG, was seen by the Europeans as usurping their role in the peace process. After intense discussions a compromise arrangement was drawn up. The secretariat of the World Bank in Paris was chosen as the headquarters for guiding operations in this sphere, but its work is supervised by an ad hoc liaison committee composed of the United States, Russia, Japan, the European Union, Canada, and Norway with Egypt, Israel, Jordan, the PLO, Saudi Arabia, Tunisia and the United Nations as associate members. The ad hoc liaison committee is formally part of the multilateral framework and reports directly on its activities to the regional economic development working group and the Steering Group. Norway, as chair of the committee, is also a member of the REDWG monitoring committee.

The European Union has taken the lead in encouraging the regional parties to explore ideas about the future long-term nature of their economic relations and to develop a vision of potential institutional mechanisms and frameworks to support and sustain their efforts towards regional cooperation. As a preliminary step in this direction the European Union convened an informal session at the end of the Rome meeting to allow regional parties to air their views. At the plenary meeting in Rabat,[2] the regional parties agreed upon a number of guidelines and principles to guide their work in the future. Specifically, they recognized the need for: (1) the pooling of common capacities and the joint tackling of common problems through coordinated efforts; (2) the removing of obstacles to a more prominent role for the private sector; (3) the promotion of regional trade, the facilitating of investment and the development of infrastructure; and (4) the encouragement of the free flow of people, goods, services, capital and information within the region. The working group also agreed in Rabat to establish a smaller monitoring committee which would be staffed by parties from the region. The aim in setting up this committee was to allow the core regional parties – Egypt, Israel, Jordan and the Palestinians – to take a more direct role in implementing the Copenhagen Action Plan, in organizing the various sectoral activities and in developing a set of priorities and identifying future projects for the working group. Initially the committee was due to convene in Cairo at the end of July. However, a series of procedural delays and disagreements surrounding its exact composition led to a postponement of the meeting and it was not until the beginning of December that the members of the monitoring committee sat down formally for the first time.[3]

During that preliminary meeting, an embryonic institutional framework governing the work of the monitoring committee was drawn up. It was agreed that the committee would comprise the four core regional parties (Egypt, Israel, Jordan and the Palestinians), the European Union (as gavel-holder), the United States and Russia (as co-sponsors of the peace process), Japan (as gavel-holder for environment), Canada (as gavel-holder for refugees), Saudi Arabia (representing the GCC), Tunisia (representing the UMA) and Norway (as chair of the ad hoc liaison committee).[4]

It was also agreed that the committee would be jointly chaired by the core regional participants and by the European Union. The regional parties' co-chairmanship would be held for six months and would rotate alphabetically, with Egypt assuming the chair on 1 January 1995. In July, Israel offered to forgo its chairmanship in favour of Jordan to ensure a greater level of coordination between the work of the monitoring committee and the preparations for the second Middle East and North Africa economic summit which was held in Amman at the end of October 1995. At the meeting of the monitoring committee in Brussels in December 1995 the core parties decided to revise the order for the chairing of the committee. In order to facilitate the setting-up of the secretariat of the monitoring committee in Amman, Jordan will retain the regional co-chairmanship for the first six months of 1996; Egypt will resume its chairmanship for the second half of the year in preparation for the third Middle East and North Africa economic summit, due to be held in Cairo; Israel will then co-chair the work of the committee during the first six months of 1997 and the Palestinians for the second half of that year.

The specific work of the monitoring committee was divided among four sectoral committees whose membership has been confined to the four core regional parties. The chairing of these committees has been shared out, with Egypt taking on responsibility for work on finance and Israel for trade; Jordan is in charge of promoting regional infrastructure, while the Palestinians chair the committee on tourism. It was also decided to appoint an executive secretary, provided by the European Union, and to establish a secretariat, to be based and staffed by personnel from the region, to service the work of the monitoring committee and the four sectoral committees. Reaching agreement among the regional parties on the permanent location of the secretariat proved to be much harder, and nearly a year passed before they all agreed that it would be based permanently in Amman. In practice, however, the secretariat, with a small skeleton staff of three people, has been operating out of Amman since March 1995 and, despite the lack of personnel, the organizational and substantive focus of the REDWG's work during the past year has shifted significantly to the secretariat and the four sectoral committees.

The sectoral committee on finance

From its inception the members of the finance committee have devoted their time and energy to advocating the cause of a regional development bank for the Middle East.[5] At the committee's first meeting, on 5 December 1994 in Cairo, the parties were determined upon a common regional approach, believing that the case for a development bank would be strengthened if the region spoke with one voice. As part of this strategy, the finance committee decided that it should seek an invitation, and make a presentation in its own right, to the Washington conference of 10 January 1995 which had been called by the United States to discuss the proposed bank.

Throughout the year the finance committee presented an unwavering and concerted regional position to the task force meetings which had been set up by the Washington conference. In a remarkable display of regional unity the members of the finance committee travelled to Bonn, London and Paris in the middle of June in an effort, ultimately unsuccessful, to persuade Germany, Britain and France respectively to alter their stance and support the setting up of a regional bank.[6] After the Amman economic summit, where it was announced that a Bank for Economic Cooperation and Development in the Middle East and North Africa would be established in Cairo, the finance committee has continued to work with the task force on the distribution of the shares, and on the drafting of the final articles of the new Bank.[7]

The sectoral committee on infrastructure

The work of the infrastructure committee covers a wide range of initiatives in railways, roads, civil aviation, maritime transport, telecommunications, electricity, and oil and gas development. The large number and the complexity of projects under discussion make it essential that these activities are carefully coordinated and monitored. To ensure such coordination and the active involvement of the regional parties in the management of these initiatives, steering committees comprising representatives of the governments directly concerned have been established to oversee the Middle East regional transport study, the integration of the region's electricity grids, the Taba–Eilat–Aqaba macro area (TEAM-A), and southeast Mediterranean economic development (SEMED).

Transport

In the early rounds of the REDWG a number of workshops were organized by France, the shepherd for this theme in the Copenhagen Action Plan, and by the European Commission, which succeeded in identifying areas for future joint ventures within the transport sector. In May 1994 a workshop on transport in the Middle East was held in Paris which focused on the importance of transport issues in economic development and identified the existing barriers to the movement of peoples and goods in the region. This was followed by two further workshops: on road transport regulation, held in Paris in October 1994, and on regional road infrastructure, held in Cairo at the same time. France and the European Commission have organized three further workshops in 1995: on ports and maritime transport (Marseilles, March 1995), on civil aviation (Toulouse, April 1995) and on railways (Paris, May 1995). The United States also hosted a workshop in January 1995 which discussed the findings of its study on air communications and the integration of regional air navigation systems in the Middle East.

Building on these various studies, the infrastructure committee, with the support of the European Commission, is currently preparing a Middle East regional transport study. The study will develop a model to forecast traffic flows in the region for the years 2010 and 2020 and will serve as a basis for the identification of and future investment in regional transport projects. The committee is also planning to hold a workshop in Amman aimed at developing further a regional strategy in the transport sector.[8] The workshop, encompassing all modes of transport, will be structured around the idea of developing traffic corridors in an integrated manner.

At the same time, the committee has identified and agreed upon the criteria for a number of 'fast-track' projects which are not dependent on the overall outcome of the study. Fast-track projects are not expected to require investment of over $30 million or to require complex institutional support. They should be easy to implement and not take more than three to four years to complete. The implementation of such projects would offer a significant boost to the working group and would help build confidence in the peace process. At the Amman economic summit three fast-track projects were presented for funding: the Jordan river crossing point (also known as Sheikh Hussein Bridge) linking Israel with Jordan; King Hussein Bridge (also known as the Allenby Bridge) connecting Jordan and the West Bank; and the Rafah crossing point between Egypt and Gaza.

Energy

Austria, with the support of the European Commission, organized a workshop in Aqaba in December 1994 and has produced a feasibility study on interconnecting electricity grids in the region. During a further workshop held in Haifa on 27–28 September 1995 the parties established a steering committee and a regional office to oversee this project. The project has reached the planning stage and a detailed feasibility study has been commissioned from the European Commission by the Jordan Electricity Authority which is acting as the regional coordinator for this initiative. As part of the regional framework, a national electricity grid will be established to serve the Palestinians.

A pre-feasibility study, produced by Italy, has examined the economic potential of a natural gas pipeline which would connect Egypt, Gaza and Israel. The committee has also discussed possible areas of cooperation in oil and gas development and renewable energy sources.

Telecommunications

Cooperation in the field of telecommunications is still at an early stage. The first workshop in this field was held in Tel Aviv on 11–12 December 1995. The workshop discussed various telecommunications networks and the development of a Middle East telecommunications superhighway to enable the peoples of the region to participate in the much-vaunted global information society.

Integrated development programmes

In addition to the work being undertaken on specific projects, the infrastructure committee has identified three sub-regions for programmes of integrated economic development: the Gulf of Aqaba, the east Mediterranean coast and the Jordan rift valley. Work on developing these initiatives will be conducted in close coordination with the other relevant multilateral working groups.

The Taba–Eilat–Aqaba–macro area (TEAM-A)

The steering committee of this programme is developing a common regional approach to the development of the northern Aqaba region. The overall planning approach focuses on strengthening the infrastructural links between Egypt, Israel and Jordan, coordinating environmental protection and attracting private-sector investment to the area. The future economic development of the area will centre on regional tourism, modern transport services and new industrial and trade activities.

The southeast Mediterranean economic development (SEMED) programme

This programme involves Egyptians, Palestinians and Israelis and covers the El-Arish–Gaza–Ashdod area. The aim of SEMED is to develop projects that have cross-border benefits and that can be readily implemented. The steering committee for this initiative held its first meeting in Cairo on 19–20 September 1995 and agreed upon a vision statement for the area for the year 2020:

> An efficient and competitive Mediterranean Community providing high quality agricultural, industrial, leisure and tourism products and services to international markets; gaining high levels of employment and income for all of its people; and securing environmentally sustainable economic growth based on the efficient use of available resources.

The Jordan rift valley plan

The aim of this multi-sector, cross-border development plan is to provide infrastructure and services to support private-sector-led growth in the area. Originally conceived as a bilateral initiative with the objective of consolidating peace between Israel and Jordan, the aim now is to expand the scheme to a broader multilateral framework. Specific plans for the area include new and improved transport and telecommunications links, the promotion of tourism, the management of shared natural resources, and joint research into earth sciences and desert agriculture.

The sectoral committee on trade

The Middle East regional business council

One of the first tasks facing the trade committee was to promote work on establishing a Middle East regional business council, another of the institutions called for at the end of the Casablanca economic summit. The council was officially launched one year later at the Amman economic summit. The committee, with the assistance of the United States, commissioned a report to identify the specific services such an organization might provide to the business community of the region. On the basis of this report a task force consisting of the REDWG trade committee and representatives of the regional business community was set up to oversee the establishment of the council, to draft a charter and a set of bylaws, to make detailed arrangements for the appointment of an executive director and staff, and to mobilize resources and prepare an initial three-year budget for the council.

The council will be a private non-profit organization drawing its membership and board of governors from the regional business community. Its aim will be to encourage trade and investment in the Middle East by assisting in the creation of a strong, healthy business environment, by promoting and developing business and investment opportunities, and by providing a forum for the exchange of information and views of mutual interest to the business communities of the region.

Trade studies

The German government, which is the shepherd for trade promotion within the region, has commissioned a number of studies. The Institute for Economic Research (IFO) in Munich has published a study on *New Potentials for Cooperation and Trade in the Middle East* which focuses on trade in goods and services. A related study, *Measures to Facilitate the Free Flow of Trade within the Middle East*, has been produced by the German–Arab chamber of commerce in Cairo. This report analyses specific examples of obstacles to trade within the Middle East and provides a series of practical suggestions to overcome these impediments.

At the REDWG plenary meeting in Bonn, the Swiss government announced that it was setting up a small team of experts, headed by Arthur Dunkel, the former director-general of GATT, to look at the prospects for regional economic integration in the Middle East. The aim of this initiative, called the Swiss Trade Initiative Middle East and North Africa (STIMENA) is to examine possible ways of establishing a framework conducive to trade liberalization and to stimulating competition, financial flows, private investment and technology transfer within the region. In the middle of December 1995, STIMENA organized a round-table discussion in Geneva, in which the REDWG trade committee participated with the aim of reviewing the various trade studies and developing practical recommendations on how these studies might be implemented.

The sectoral committee on tourism

The Middle East and Mediterranean Travel and Tourism Association

Japan has taken responsibility for promoting tourism in the region and has played a pivotal role, with the tourism committee, in setting up a new regional tourism body, the Middle East and Mediterranean Travel and Tourism Association (MEMTTA). Throughout 1995 it organized a series of workshops in the region during which the charter for this new organization was drawn up. The charter of the association was initialled on 28 September 1995 in Casablanca and was signed during the Amman economic summit.

The aim of MEMTTA is to promote and market the Middle East as a destination for tourists and to assist in the development of local tourist industries. It is intended that it will act as an instrument in developing close collaboration between the public and private sectors on tourism issues and help integrate the region into the global marketing system. It will also provide for training in tourism services and encourage the harmonization of laws and regulations relating to tourism. One of the most urgent tasks facing the association is to identify ways of easing the movement of tourists within the region.

Training

One of the priorities for the expansion of tourism in the region is to improve the training capabilities of the tourist industry and services. The Swiss government has produced a report on hotel training which makes a number of specific recommendations and identifies a need at the higher management level for a regional approach to the training of personnel. The report also recommends that exchange visits should be arranged among the existing regional training institutions.

In October 1994 the United States organized a workshop in Cairo for tour operators at which nine leading US tour operators briefed over 100 regional government and private-sector tourism representatives. A similar workshop for European and Middle Eastern tour operators took place in Aqaba in January 1995.

Other activities and projects within the Copenhagen Action Plan

Agriculture (Spain)

Spain has sent several missions of experts to the region to assess the potential for agricultural development and has produced a report on *Agricultural Development in the Middle East in a Regional Context*. One of the specific recommendations in the report is the creation of a regional cooperation agency through which the regional parties can openly discuss and develop joint action programmes. The European Commission has been examining veterinary issues and animal health. It has organized a workshop of veterinary officials aimed at drawing up a list of proposals for creating collaborative networks for joint vaccination and other disease control systems.

Financial markets and investment (United Kingdom)

As part of its activities as shepherd in this field, the United Kingdom hosted a conference organized by the Royal Institute of International Affairs on financial markets in the Middle East at the end of April 1994. It has also completed a study examining areas of potential cooperation between stock exchanges in the region which it presented to the plenary meeting in Bonn.

Public health (Italy)

This is a new sector within the Copenhagen Action Plan which was proposed by Italy at the meeting in Rabat. Italy is carrying out an assessment of health technology throughout the region. It is also conducting, in conjunction with UNICEF, an assessment of the training needs for Palestinian health managers and is devising a programme for the setting-up of a national health services management unit for the Palestinians, aimed at strengthening health services at hospital and primary-care level.

Training (United States)

The United States serves as shepherd for training initiatives, and many of the activities undertaken in this field have been carried out in conjunction with the water, environment and refugee working groups. Germany has prepared a study on *Regional Labour Market Orientated Training* and has organized a conference on this subject in Heidelberg at the end of May 1995.

Networks (European Union)

The European Union has taken on the responsibility for creating a series of networks between cities, universities and the media in Israel, Jordan, Egypt and the West Bank and Gaza. A conference was held in Cairo on 13–15 December 1993 to launch this initiative, following which contracts were drawn up for the Peace-URBS (cities), Peace-CAMPUS (universities) and Peace-MEDIA (media) networks. A follow-up conference for these three networks was held in Aqaba in March 1995.

Bibliography (Canada)

Canada has published two literature surveys on economic cooperation and integration in the Middle East. The first survey was produced in collaboration with Israeli, Palestinian and Jordanian research centres. The second volume includes sources of information produced by or specializing on Egypt.

The future of the REDWG

The range and extent of the activities of the REDWG monitoring committee mark a qualitative and quantitative change in the role of the working group. The establishment of the monitoring committee and the secretariat represents a significant step in transferring the responsibility of managing and driving the process of economic cooperation to the region itself. The four core parties – Israel, Jordan, Egypt and the Palestinians – have not been found wanting in this task: through their work in the sectoral committees, they have been instrumental in framing a set of priorities for the REDWG, and in developing a defined, coherent strategy to meet those goals. New principles, norms and patterns of behaviour are being forged. The monitoring committee, its four sectoral committees and the secretariat reflect the first tentative steps towards the fashioning of new common structures of cooperation, coordination and decision-making in the Middle East.

The REDWG now faces a number of challenges in building on the achievements of the past four years. Notably, the working group needs to move from the planning stage to the implementation of specific projects so that the rewards of economic cooperation are visible to the peoples of the region. This will require the mobilization of financial resources and will inevitably necessitate a greater involvement of the private sector in the activities and proceedings of the working group in the long run. As it is, there are many more projects under consideration than there are funds to implement them. In addition, the parties need to focus on strengthening the institutionalization of the process of regional economic cooperation in the Middle East. After a year of uncertainty, the regional parties finally agreed at the Amman economic summit that the secretariat of the monitoring committee should be transformed into a permanent regional economic institution which would be based in the Jordanian capital. The Amman summit also entrusted the core regional parties with drawing up the framework and operational functions of this institution, and preliminary discussions to that effect were held during the meeting of the monitoring committee in Brussels at the end of the year.

Great skill will be needed in this task. The past year has witnessed the emergence of a host of new regional economic frameworks: the Bank for Economic Cooperation and Development in the Middle East and North Africa, with its Forum for Economic Cooperation, the Middle East–Mediterranean Travel and Tourism Association, and the Middle East Business Council. Little attention has been paid, however, to their interrelationships or to how these new frameworks will complement each other in promoting and strengthening regional economic cooperation.

The experience of the peace process during the past four years reveals not a lack of multilateralism but rather too much multilateralism in the economic sphere. These new frameworks run the danger of ending up as competing and not complementary mechanisms, reflecting the conflicting bilateral agendas of both the regional and the extra-regional parties.

The process of regional economic cooperation in the Middle East demands not only the resolve and commitment of the regional parties themselves but also the active participation of the international community in support of those endeavours. International assistance and financial support are essential for the development of the individual economies on the domestic front as well as in terms of the whole region. The multilateral talks have witnessed the commitment of the international community to securing a comprehensive and lasting resolution to the Arab–Israeli conflict and the valuable role of outside partners, acting as catalysts, for the regional parties. The REDWG has fostered a unique partnership between the international community and the countries of the region in fostering the conditions for a new era of regional cooperation in the Middle East. Ultimately, however, the responsibility for shaping priorities, for developing strategies and for setting the pace of regional economic cooperation lies with the regional parties. The experience of the monitoring committee indicates that they are ready to shoulder that responsibility. But it is equally important that the evolving structures for economic cooperation, and in particular the operating framework of the secretariat, succeed in maintaining the spirit of partnership developed in the REDWG. Hitherto, the extra-regional players have exercised a greater measure of control, including over the allocation of funds, than they will do in the future as the initiative is passed to the region. Consequently, it will be necessary to ensure that this transition does not result in the distancing and the disengagement of the international community from the process. Finding the right balance will not be easy, but this is the challenge now facing all the parties concerned.

9 EVALUATION AND THE FUTURE OF THE MULTILATERALS

The multilateral talks have been the hidden dimension of the Arab–Israeli peace process. Over the past four years attention has been focused almost exclusively on the series of bilateral negotiations between Israel and its immediate Arab neighbours. Reports about developments in the multilateral track have been scarce and uninformative. As a result, there is little awareness of the nature of these talks or of the issues under discussion. The absence of interest has been mistakenly equated with a lack of significance. Although the multilateral talks do not carry the same immediacy and importance as the questions at the heart of the bilaterals, they have nonetheless, and contrary to all expectations, performed a valuable role in the peace process and in fostering the conditions for future cooperative arrangements in the Middle East. A number of conceptual developments and specific achievements can be identified.

The importance of informality

It is true that much of the progress made in the multilateral talks cannot be translated into any immediate or identifiable impact on the daily lives of the people in the region. Large parts of the talks, especially during the early rounds, have concentrated on procedural rather than substantive issues. Considerable time and energy were devoted to questions of participation and representation in these talks, especially in respect of the composition of the Palestinian delegation. The participation of all (the then) twelve member states of the European Union in the arms control talks, for example, was not accepted until the fifth round of talks and the United Nations has only recently become involved in the activities of the multilaterals. Consensus has been achieved around the agendas for discussion, over the areas for information–gathering and feasibility studies, and in the willingness of the parties to participate in a variety of workshops and inter-sessional activities. The talks have only just reached the stage of assessing the detail and the implementation of specific projects.

While Israel and the Arab states have been formally sitting around the table in the multilaterals, many of the activities undertaken have resembled the functions usually associated with the pre-negotiation phase in a negotiation process. Pre-negotiation has been defined as 'the span of time and activity in which the parties move from conflicting unilateral solutions for a mutual problem to a joint search for cooperative or joint solutions'. Pre-negotiation represents a transformation and a redefining of relationships; it denotes a shift in thinking from a conflictual stance to one of potential cooperation. The pre-negotiation phase is a 'purposive period of transition that enables parties to move from conflicting perceptions and behaviours (unilateral attempts at solutions) to cooperative perceptions and behaviours'.[1] In this respect the multilateral talks have provided the framework, have set the boundaries and have helped in shaping the 'rules of the game' for the conduct of future negotiations between Israel and the Arab world. They have identified a number of common problems, have determined the eligibility of the participants and have drawn up agendas for discussion.

During the multilateral talks over the past four years Israel and the Arab states have not been engaged in a process of bargaining whereby, if successful, they will eventually converge incrementally, via a series of mutual concessions, on an agreed outcome. But negotiation should not be seen as simply a sequence of concessions, or a matter of deciding how much each side will give and take. Rather, it is a 'process of discovery which leads to some degree of reorganization and adjustment of understanding, expectations and behaviour, leading (if successful) eventually to more specific discussion about possible terms of a final, agreed outcome'.[2] It is a process of defining and redefining a conflictual relationship comprising a series of stages whereby the parties move from problem recognition to problem-solving.[3]

The multilateral track differs fundamentally from the bilateral talks in its approach to the resolution of the Arab–Israeli conflict. The multilateral talks and the inter-sessional activities have resembled an exercise in 'track two diplomacy' and the 'problem-solving workshop' approach to conflict resolution. Track two diplomacy has been defined as unofficial, informal interaction between members of adversarial groups or nations which aims to develop strategies, influence public opinion and organize human and material resources in ways that might help resolve their conflict. It is a process designed to assist official leaders to resolve or, in the first instance, to manage conflicts by exploring possible solutions away from the public view and without the requirement to negotiate formally or bargain for advantage.[4] Track two diplomacy has been seen as an alternative to formal contacts between states and has stressed the importance of unofficial, non-structured interaction involving participants who are not government representatives. The experience of the multilateral talks, however, indicates the value and the applicability of this approach at the governmental level, especially in a region characterized by deep-rooted and long-standing conflict.

Summary of achievements

Effective negotiation requires preparation, learning, understanding and support. It is severely hampered in an environment of mistrust, selective and distorted perceptions, negative attitudes, poor communication and a competitive win-lose, zero-sum situation exemplified in the Arab–Israeli conflict. The multilaterals have provided a unique forum for low-risk communication and exchanges between Israel and the Arabs. Participation in these talks and the inter-sessional workshops has afforded the parties an opportunity to evaluate the feasibility of future cooperative arrangements, generate ideas for creative solutions and determine the basis of future activities. Because they receive little media coverage, those involved can test out new general approaches or specific ideas without making any formal public commitment. The talks and related activities have allowed Israel and the Arab states to acquire new sources of information which may change positively their perceptions and attitudes. They have helped them to rethink their old assumptions, reduce their fear of risk and uncertainty, and explore possibilities for joint problem-solving. They have presented an opportunity for each side to gain an insight into the goals and intentions, the perceptions and anxieties, the flexibility and limits of the other. These insights may in turn affect their ideas about what is feasible, necessary and promising in the search for common solutions. For the first time these states have been willing to address common problems in a non-confrontational atmosphere and to think and plan in regional terms.

An additional benefit is that the more collegial atmosphere can help negotiators develop personal contacts and working relationships, mutual understandings and empathy with the views of others, which may facilitate negotiations at a later stage.[5] Although these seemingly nebulous by-products of the multilateral talks are difficult to measure, they should not be cursorily dismissed.

The multilaterals have also provided a mechanism for the development of bilateral relations between the Israeli government and its Arab counterparts. Only the few are involved in the bilateral negotiations, and prior to Madrid, aside from Egypt, the Arab states had never participated in direct talks or official contacts with Israel. On the contrary, they were officially at war. It is the multilaterals which have allowed the Gulf states, most notably Bahrain, Qatar and Oman, and the North African states of Tunisia and Morocco, to become engaged in the peace process. These states have been prepared to host the plenary sessions of the multilaterals with the full and open participation of Israel, a prospect which would have seemed unimaginable only a few years ago, and to play an active role in many of the inter-sessional activities. This has led to a series of open bilateral meetings between Israeli ministers and their Arab counterparts and the development of diplomatic ties between Israel and the Arab world. Israel has opened diplomatic interest offices with Morocco and Tunisia, and agreement has been reached for the reciprocal exchange of commercial missions with Oman.

Another important spin-off from the multilaterals has been the gradual erosion of the Arab boycott of Israel, resulting in the formal announcement by the GCC states of the end of the secondary and tertiary boycott of Israel and the development of commercial ties between Israel and the Gulf states.[6] The convening of the Middle East–North Africa economic summit in Casablanca at the end of October 1994, and the follow-up summit in Amman one year later, together with the creation of a new regional development bank for the Middle East, are further signs of the emergence of a new regional order and the willingness of the states of the region to enter into new joint collaborative ventures with Israel. Although these initiatives are not directly a part of the multilaterals, they are clearly a by-product of the multilateral track as a whole.

The importance of the widening of the peace process to include the broader Arab world cannot be overestimated, especially in the context of the domestic political environment within Israel. The pictures of Israeli delegations being openly and warmly greeted in the Gulf and North Africa have served to strengthen the hand of the Israeli government.[7] The presence of leaders from the Arab world, including the Prime Minister of Morocco, the Foreign Minister of Oman, and representatives from Qatar and Tunisia, at the funeral of Yitzhak Rabin left an indelible mark on the minds of the Israeli public.

The regional dimension of the peace process has developed an increasing significance with the renewal of talks between Israel and Syria at the end of 1995. The intention of the Israeli government under the leadership of Shimon Peres is to link an Israeli withdrawal from the Golan Heights and the signing of a peace agreement with Syria with the full normalization of relations with the broader Arab world. Peres' aim is to present the Israeli electorate with the opportunity of voting for a 'regional peace' and for finally ending the cycle of conflict between Israel and all the Arab states. What was previously dismissed as political wishful thinking has come to assume a central role in Israel's new diplomatic strategy.[8]

From the outset there was a recognition by all sides that progress in the multilateral talks was dependent upon developments on the bilateral stage. There was an acceptance that no agreements, however limited in scope, could be reached or implemented prior to a significant breakthrough in the bilateral talks. Although potential mutually beneficial arrangements might emerge from discussions in the multilateral meetings, there was no expectation that these talks would substitute for agreements at the bilateral level. Yet the multilaterals have played an important complementary role to the bilateral talks. They have defined a valuable division of labour and separation of issues, by providing a forum for the discussion of areas that are primarily technical in nature and separable from the primary issues at stake but that nevertheless might impede negotiations and create stumbling blocks to the achievement of a full settlement.

The multilateral track has also allowed the parties to attend to long-term issues which need to be addressed if and when a settlement is reached. Without them it would not have been possible to develop collectively some concepts for regional economic, social and cultural relations in the aftermath of years of war. Such long-term thinking and planning cannot take place in the context of the bilateral negotiations, which are inevitably governed by more immediately pressing concerns. It is in this contribution to the post-settlement phase of the Arab–Israeli peace process that the real importance of the multilaterals lies.

In fact, many of the issues under discussion in the multilateral talks are as much bilateral as they are multilateral. The multilaterals have allowed the parties to discuss these issues and to propose ideas which at a later stage might be fed back into the bilateral arena when they become relevant to the proceedings. For instance, the multilaterals have offered an alternative forum for addressing the future of the Palestinians of Gaza and the West Bank. It was during the second round of the multilaterals that Palestinians from outside the territories, who had been excluded under the rules of the Madrid conference, were first allowed to participate in the peace process. Also, a number of the inter-sessional activities and projects have focused on the infrastructural development needs of the occupied territories and have provided for the training of Palestinian personnel. Most notably, it was through the REDWG talks that the World Bank was commissioned to produce a report on the economy of the occupied territories. It is this report which now serves as the basis for many of the ideas currently under discussion for the development of Gaza and the West Bank and for the directing of aid pledged by the international community to the Palestinians. Similarly, many of the provisions included in the Declaration of Principles and the annexes to that document, such as a Palestinian environmental authority and a Palestinian water administration authority, were first aired in the multilaterals.

This kind of spillover effect has been apparent in other facets of the bilaterals. For example, many of the provisions of the Israeli–Jordanian peace treaty, especially in the area of water, were first raised in the multilateral talks. It is particularly noteworthy in this respect that the head of the Jordanian delegation to the working group on water was also one of the principal negotiators of the Israeli–Jordanian peace treaty. Indeed, although Syria and Lebanon have not been party to the multilaterals, much of the discussions and the understandings arrived at in the multilaterals in the realm of water, environment and economic cooperation will facilitate negotiations between Israel and those two countries when the time is propitious.

Breaking down issues into narrowly defined functional areas and bringing together experts from regional and extra-regional parties allows opinions, concerns and potential alternative solutions to be raised. The multilaterals have led to the emergence of a number of 'epistemic communities', defined as 'a network of professionals with recognized expertise and competence in a particular domain and an authoritative claim to policy relevant knowledge within that domain,'[9] which may affect decisions at the policy level. This was noted by the former US Assistant Secretary of State, Edward Djerejian, in his observations on the Working Group on the Environment:

> The mode of operation has been to bring experts – not politicians or diplo-mats – from the region together at workshops and set them to addressing the problems. What we found was that when we put these experts together they solved problems. Beyond the glare of the political klieg lights, we created an environment where scientists spoke a common language.[10]

Continuous interaction between specialists from the different countries can, over time foster a convergence of expectations and the institutionalization of norms of behaviour, and this is not restricted to experts in the various technical fields. Through the multilateral process, the states of the Middle East are beginning to develop a set of principles, norms, rules and decision-making procedures to govern the nature of their relations in the future. The Working Group on the Environment has drawn up the Bahrain Environmental Code of Conduct for the Middle East, while the efforts of the parties in the 'conceptual basket' of the ACRS working group have been engaged in drafting a Declaration of Principles.

Yet, in this respect progress has been difficult to achieve across the board. At the inter-sessional meeting of the Steering Group in Montebello the parties correctly recognized that the multilateral track should not be concerned solely with the accumulation of projects but that it needs to develop a strategic vision and a set of principles to guide the process of regional cooperation in the Middle East. The Steering Group was entrusted with the drafting of a guidelines paper for the multilateral process and the gavel-holders were instructed to produce 'vision papers' for their respective working groups. Although a timetable was drawn up at the meeting of the Steering Group in Tabarka for the drafting of these papers, little thought was given to the overall objective and to how this initiative would be coordinated and managed. Although draft vision papers, of varying length and substance, were produced in time for the Steering Group meeting in Montreux, little headway has been made during the past two years in bringing this exercise to a successful conclusion. There was no more than minimal discussion of the vision papers in Montreux, since when the parties have only intermittently turned their minds to this subject. The neglect of this exercise belies the importance of bringing the parties together to address the long-term objectives of the multilateral track and of developing a set of principles to guide the process in the future. The Steering Group needs to return to this question with a greater sense of priority and invest the appropriate time and resources that this initiative warrants and demands.

Meantime, in terms of functional issues, the multilaterals are laying the groundwork for the emergence of a new set of regional institutions such as the desalination research centre in Oman, the environmental training centres in Jordan and Bahrain, and the proposed regional security centre in Amman. Of particular significance is the establishment within the REDWG of the monitoring committee and the decision to set up a permanent secretariat in Amman. The creation of this secretariat represents an important and qualitative step in the institutionalization of the multilateral process, and in transferring the responsibility for driving the process of regional cooperation to the regional parties themselves.

Concerted efforts towards new forms of regional cooperation in the Middle East require the development of more and sustainable institutional arrangements. Institutions not only facilitate the effectiveness of activities in this sphere but are also important in developing new norms and patterns of behaviour. So far, the majority of the discussions in the multilaterals have been characterized by their informal nature. Without doubt this has contributed significantly to the development and the success of these talks to date: the emphasis has been deliberately placed on loose frameworks; bargaining has been exploratory and communication relatively free. However, with the desire to reach agreements this loose process is likely to sharpen as discussions proceed. Obligations will become firmer, formulas and definitions will crystallize and trade-offs will become clearer and more urgent. As discussions move away from the feasibility of ideas towards the implementation of specific projects, they will begin less to resemble academic seminars and more to take on the form of adversarial bargaining between political units. In those conditions the consensual arrangements achieved during the past four years will come under severe pressure. The development of an institutional framework is therefore important in helping to mediate and contain these potential conflicts of interest and in reinforcing the process of regional cooperation.

The informal, low-key nature of the multilateral meetings, combined with the absence of expectations surrounding them, has without doubt contributed significantly to the developments and achievements of the multilateral track. This informality which lies at the heart of the multilateral process has been its great strength. At the same time, and as a consequence, this has resulted in a process lacking in focus and direction. Although the Steering Group was set up to oversee and coordinate the activities of the multilaterals, it has not executed this role fully. At the two inter-sessional meetings of the Steering Group in Montebello (February 1994) and Cairo (January 1995), the parties acknowledged the neccesity of providing the multilaterals with a greater sense of strategic management and direction. However, they have failed to achieve this. The Steering Group last met in May 1995 and on that occasion the bulk of its proceedings was devoted to discussing the question of Jerusalem rather than the future direction and objectives of the multilateral process itself.

Time to take stock

A number of issues, many of them interrelated, now require attention. The first centres on the allocation of resources and implementation of specific projects. It was always the hope that the multilaterals would serve to marshal the experience, expertise and financial resources of the international community in order to underwrite the peace process. In this the multilateral talks have been extremely successful. They have witnessed the commitment of the international community to securing the foundations of a durable settlement to the Arab–Israeli conflict and the economic development of the region. This has been reflected in the increasing level of participation of non-regional actors in the multilateral talks, their willingness to host meetings, to act as 'shepherds' and provide funding for the inter-sessional activities. However, though the range and variety of projects looks impressive on paper, many of these activities have yet to progress beyond the planning stages. In many cases the projects require a greater level of public funding than is readily available. There is a growing need to draw up a list of priorities, to ensure that expectations are not raised unrealistically and that projects which cannot be adequately financed are not pursued. Above all, ways must found to incorporate the private sector in the activities of the multilateral working groups and in the development of specific projects. The provision of adequate financial resources for projects devised within the multilaterals was not thought out sufficiently at the launching of this process, nor has it been adequately addressed since. The allocation of financial resources and a rationalization of the number of projects are crucial if the multilaterals are not to become simply a talking-shop and a market-place for false hopes and promises.

The second set of issues relates to the more efficient and effective use of existing resources. In particular, the parties need to consider the creation of more formal institutional mechanisms to oversee and coordinate the various activities within the framework of the multilaterals. There is a considerable degree of duplication in many of the projects and inter-sessional meetings of the water, environment, refugee and regional economic development working groups. Frequently ideas have been raised in one group with little awareness of similar discussions in other working groups or of how these projects might complement other activities in the multilaterals.[11] The whole process has become unwieldy and suffers not from a lack of, but rather from a surfeit of multilateral endeavours. Paradoxically, despite the loose, informal nature of the multilaterals and the lack of any overall blueprint at the outset, the architecture and operating structure that has evolved gradually over the past four years has developed into a rigid and inflexible edifice. As a result, it has become increasingly difficult to incorporate new ideas and issues which sit uneasily within the existing framework. Efforts to rationalize and coordinate the various activities have become the victim of competing bilateral agendas and of the overall uncertainty surrounding the long-term objectives of the multilaterals.

The parties, however, would be ill-advised to devote their energies to significantly altering the existing framework. The benefits to be gained from such an exercise at this stage in the peace process are unlikely to outweigh the numerous difficulties. Rather, decisions over the rationalization, prioritization and funding of projects demand a more centralized and systematic management of the multilateral track. To this end, the multilateral talks should set up a permanent secretariat, staffed by the regional parties, to oversee the process more effectively. A secretariat is essential for the logistical tasks of convening meetings and developing or commissioning background documentation, and providing a continuity for talks that may stretch over a period of years during which there may be considerable turnover in personnel. The parties should look closely at the experience of the REDWG monitoring committee and the contribution of the secretariat set up to service its work. In particular, they should assess in what ways the REDWG experience might be replicated in other working groups, and consider if, and in what ways, this embryonic institutional mechanism might serve as a means of rationalizing and coordinating the work of the multilaterals as a whole.

This issue is closely allied to the question of establishing a permanent location(s) for the multilaterals. Over the past four years the multilateral talks have been hosted by a wide variety of states (see Appendix 2), but the symbolic value of choosing venues in the Middle East has been emphasized. The willingness of the international community, and especially the Arab world, to host these talks has been regarded as a sign of the commitment of all the parties, regional and non-regional, to this process. Conference locations, however, should also have a practical value. The spreading of the multilateral meetings across the globe has been a drain on the resources, human and financial, of the parties involved in these talks. Often the size of delegations has been determined by travel and financial considerations, thereby undermining the value of the meetings in their own right. The parties involved need to pay attention to such practical concerns in deciding upon the venues for future meetings.[12]

Recently, the idea of linking the plenary sessions so that they meet simultaneously in one location has been gaining currency. The first step in this direction was taken in June 1995 with the simultaneous meetings of the water and the environment working groups in Amman. Avoiding the duplication of efforts, however, requires more than simple measures of this kind. Although there is a clear overlap in the current, and future, areas of discussion of these two working groups, clustering the plenary meetings of the multilaterals may lead to a dilution rather than an increase in the effectiveness of the working groups. Over the past four years, the five working groups have developed their own dynamics, modes of operation and personnel. The parties should, however, consider strongly the setting-up of either a permanent location for the multilaterals in one of the capitals of the Middle East or a fixed venue for each of the working groups. A permanent venue or venues would ease the convening of these meetings greatly and would also help them to develop a focal point and identity.

The final set of questions revolves around the lack of information on and public awareness of the multilateral talks. Several reasons can easily be discerned for the lack of media interest. The agenda of the multilaterals does not have the same immediacy and obvious importance as the bilateral negotiations where the critical issues of the Arab–Israeli conflict – namely, territory, security and the rights of Palestinians – are being addressed. A large part of the talks has been concerned with procedural rather than substantive issues; much of the progress achieved so far does not have any identifiable or immediate consequences for the daily lives of the people in the region; and many of the issues under discussion are functional, technical and complex in nature. That said, there has been a deliberate effort by the parties to keep the publicity surrounding these talks to a minimum. The multilaterals have been designed to allow the parties to raise issues and ideas without making any formal public commitment. Bargaining has been exploratory and communication relatively free. Official minutes of the meetings have not been recorded, nor have formal closing statements been issued. Press statements have been brief and have offered few details of the agendas and issues under discussion. The multilaterals have been an exercise in diplomacy by stealth.

The informal, low-key nature of the multilateral meetings, together with the absence of expectations surrounding these talks, have without doubt contributed significantly to the development of this track. Hidden away from the glare of the international media, the results of these meetings have not been judged by the immediacy of their outcomes. But the lack of public awareness of the agendas of these talks, of the progress achieved and of the potential benefits to be accrued by future cooperation, runs contrary to one of the aims of the multilateral track, namely the creation of a set of confidence-building measures between the parties and publics of the region. Confidence-building has so far been confined to the level of elites.

The continuing semi-secret nature of these meetings is more harmful than beneficial to the future of the multilateral track. The lack of information has been accompanied by a poverty in the analysis of its role and contribution to the peace process. Press reports, infrequent as they have been, have highlighted the differences and difficulties encountered at various stages in the process, and have conveyed a negative impression of the overall value of these talks.

The multilaterals need to develop a 'trademark', a distinct and separate identity that will allow the peoples of the Middle East to understand, identify and support their objectives. Knowledge of the specific developments and projects within the working groups needs to be widened to involve a larger number of public, academic and special-interest groups – and, especially, the private sector. The lack of information and awareness has led to a disengagement of these publics from the specific activities under review. Past experience highlights the contribution of these audiences to efforts to transform Arab–Israeli relations. Their potential contribution needs to recognized by the parties, and ways should be found to incorporate them into the dynamics and complexities of the multilateral framework.

The lack of identifiable outcomes and concrete projects emerging from the multilateral talks has led many to dismiss the value and to question the continued utility of this process. In particular, there have been calls for the convening of a conference on security and cooperation in the Middle East (CSCME) modelled on the CSCE process in Europe. Indeed, Israel and Jordan, in Article 4 of their peace treaty, commit themselves to setting up such a framework. The regional parties need to look ahead and plan for future regional security structures and cooperative arrangements; a CSCME could be envisaged as one of the potential long-term outcomes of the multilateral process.[13] But it would be premature and unwise to adopt such a high-level and, inevitably, politicized approach at this stage of the peace process. Such an exercise would only undermine the benefits gained so far and put the consensual arrangements achieved to date under severe pressure. While process should not be overly confused with substance, the experience of the multilateral track points to the value, and indeed to the necessity, of maintaining a gradualist and incremental approach to the development of regional cooperation in the Middle East. The transformation of Arab–Israeli relations, after fifty years of conflict, requires a purposive period of transition to allow the parties to move towards cooperative perceptions and patterns of behaviour. Such a climate of confidence can be best generated by small steps undertaken in a pragmatic manner rather than by ambitious undertakings. The multilateral talks offer a vehicle for the discussion of proposals and for the setting-up of mechanisms which will lead to an overarching regional organization. The regional parties would be served best by strengthening the existing framework of the multilateral track and by directing it along the path of progressive institutionalization.

The multilaterals have been hampered by the absence of Syria and Lebanon and it is vital that these two countries are brought into the process to ensure that any agreements achieved are neither partial nor contested. Every effort should be made to encourage them to join the multilateral track without delay. Their boycott of these talks has not succeeded in derailing the multilateral track; but their absence has limited the scope of many of the discussions. Most of the issues and areas of future action already identified by the multilateral talks are of equal concern to the future welfare of these two states. If Syria and Lebanon joined the multilateral talks, this would be an important confidence-building measure which would boost both the bilateral and the multilateral tracks.

With all such caveats and cautions in mind, it is time to conclude on a positive note. The inclusion of the multilateral track in the Madrid process was an ambitious undertaking and one fraught with uncertainties. Yet, contrary to all expectations, the multilateral talks have performed a valuable role in moving relations between Israel and the Arabs along the path towards a new era of peace and prosperity. They have developed a wide agenda of potential projects which will link the parties together into a new set of joint ventures and cooperative arrangements. The multilaterals have not only reflected the changes within the region but have also fostered the conditions for a truly comprehensive, lasting resolution to the Arab–Israeli conflict and for the emergence of new era of regional cooperation in the Middle East.

NOTES

Chapter 2

1   For the Syrian position on the multilateral talks see Foreign Broadcasting Information Service (FBIS)/MEA, *Daily Report*, 10 May 1993, p. 5.

2   Consensus was defined by the CSCE process as 'understood to mean the absence of any objection expressed by a Representative and submitted by him as constituting an obstacle to the taking of the decision in question'. For a discussion of consensus and multilateral negotiations see Saadia Touval, 'Multilateral Negotiation: An Analytic Approach', *Negotiation Journal*, 5, 2, April 1989, pp. 169–71. On the development of decisions by consensus in the Law of Sea Conference see Barry Buzan, 'Negotiating by Consensus: Developments in Technique at the United Nations Conference on the Law of the Sea', *American Journal of International Law*, 75, 2, 1981, pp. 324–48. For an account of consensus decision-making at the Conference on Security and Cooperation in Europe (CSCE) see Jan Sizoo and Rudolf Th. Jurrjens, *CSCE Decision Making: The Madrid Experience* (The Hague: Martinus Nijhoff, 1984), pp. 49–75.

3   A certain amount of confusion surrounds the numbering of the rounds of talks. After several rounds it was decided that the organizational meeting in Moscow should be regarded as the first round of the multilaterals. However, many of the gavel-summaries and press statements issued do not describe the Moscow meeting as the first round of the multilateral talks. For the sake of clarity and consistency, this book counts the first round of talks as starting in May 1992.

Chapter 3

1   The Ad Hoc Liaison Committee was established after the donors' pledging conference on 1 October 1993 in order to promote and coordinate aid to the Palestinians in Gaza and the West Bank.

2 For Israel's contribution to this discussion see *A Vision of the Middle East* (Jerusalem: Israeli Ministry of Foreign Affairs, December 1993). For a grand vision for the future from an Israeli perspective see Shimon Peres, *The New Middle East* (Shaftesbury: Element Books, 1993). While Peres raises many ideas for future cooperation between Israel and the Arab world, he does not suggest how these ideas might be realized, nor does he discuss the multilateral talks in any detail.

3 This was not the first occasion on which the Arab states had called for the creation of a new working group on Jerusalem: they had previously raised this idea in the early meetings of the Steering Group, but not with the same vigour.

4 For reports in the Israeli press on this meeting see *Ma'ariv*, 20 May 1995, and *Ha'aretz*, 20 May 1995.

Chapter 4

1 Quoted in Miriam Lowi, 'Bridging the Gap: Transboundary Resource Disputes and the Case of West Bank Water', *International Security*, 18, 1, Summer 1993, p. 113.

2 For a discussion of the competition over water as a source of international conflict see Peter H. Gleich, 'Water and Conflict', *International Security*, 18, 1, Summer 1993, pp. 79–112. For an excellent recent study of the Jordan waters dispute and of previous efforts to promote functional arrangements see Miriam R. Lowi, *Water and Power: The Politics of a Scarce Resource in the Jordan River Basin* (Cambridge: Cambridge University Press, 1993). See also David M. Wishart, 'The Breakdown of the Johnston Negotiations over the Jordan Waters', *Middle East Studies,* 26, 4, 1990, pp. 536–46 and Sara Rueger, 'Controversial Waters: Exploitation of the Jordan River, 1950–80', *Middle East Studies*, 29, 1, 1993, pp. 53–90.

3 See Stephan Libiszewski, 'Water Disputes in the Jordan Basin Region and their Role in the Resolution of the Arab–Israeli Conflict', ENCOP Occasional Paper no. 13, 1995, Swiss Peace Foundation/Swiss Federal Institute of Technology. For the Palestinian position on the question of water rights see FBIS/MEA, *Daily Report*, 18 May 1992, p. 2, and 21 September 1992, pp. 5–7.

4 For a fuller and more developed discussion of this argument see Lowi, *Water and Power*.

Chapter 5

1 For reports on the fourth round of talks held in Cairo see FBIS/MEA, *Daily Report,* 17 November 1993, pp. 2–3, and 18 November 1993, pp. 3–4.

2 For reports of the meeting in Manama, Bahrain see FBIS/MEA, *Daily Report,* 24 October 1995, p. 7 and 26 October 1995, p. 4.

3 For an excellent study of the environmental problems in the Gulf of Aqaba see *Protecting the Gulf: A Regional Environmental Challenge* (Washington, DC: Environmental Law Institute, 1993).

4 For the full text of the Bahrain Environmental Code of Conduct for the Middle East see Appendix 3.

Chapter 6

1 This working group has focused exclusively on the question of the Palestinian refugees and has been, in practice, another forum for Israeli–Palestinian negotiations. It has not addressed the problems of non-Palestinian refugees in the region, nor the wider questions of migration patterns in the Middle East.

2 For a discussion of the Palestinian 'right to return' see Rashid Khalidi, 'Observation on Right of Return', *Journal of Palestine Studies,* 21, 2, 1992, pp. 29–40.

3 Israel also refused to participate in the first meeting of the regional and economic development working group for the same reason.

4 At the Cairo meeting Israel confirmed that Palestinian policemen and civil servants of the Palestine National Authority, together with their families, coming from outside Gaza and Jericho as part of the 4 May 1994 Gaza-Jericho agreement, would not be counted as part of this annual quota.

5 See Jeffrey Z. Rubin, 'Third-Party Roles: Mediation in International Environmental Disputes', in Gunnar Sjostedt (ed.), *International Environmental Negotiation* (London: Sage, 1993), pp. 275–90, and Jacob Bercovitch, 'Mediators and Mediation Strategies in International Relations', *Negotiation Journal,* April 1992, pp. 99–112.

Chapter 7

1 There has been a growing literature in recent years on arms control and the Middle East, much of it arising from a number of track two meetings and academic conferences on this issue. Two recent books are particularly

noteworthy for raising a number of important ideas on how to advance the process of arms control in the region. See Steven L. Spiegel and David J. Pervin (eds), *Practical Peacemaking in the Middle East: Arms Control and Regional Security* (New York: Garland, 1995) and Robert Eisendorf (ed.), *Arms Control and Security in the Middle East: The Search for Common Ground* (Washington, DC: The Initiative for Peace and Cooperation in the Middle East, 1995). For an excellent discussion on cooperative security and the Middle East see Robert Bowker, *Beyond Security: The Search for Security in the Middle East* (Boulder: Lynne Rienner, forthcoming 1996). For earlier discussions see Alan Platt (ed.), *Arms Control and Confidence Building in the Middle East* (Boulder: Westview, 1990); Avi Beker, *Arms Control Without Glasnost: Building Confidence in the Middle East* (Jerusalem: Israel Council of Foreign Relations, 1993); and Steven L. Spiegel, *The Arab-Israeli Search for Peace* (Boulder: Lynne Rienner, 1992).

2   See Geoffrey Kemp and Shelley A. Stahl, *The Control of the Middle East Arms Race*, (Washington, DC: Carnegie Endowment for International Peace, 1991), pp. 15–46 and 131–48.

3   For a discussion of the differing approaches of Israel and the Arab states on this question see Eisendorf (ed.), *Arms Control and Security in the Middle East: The Search for Common Ground;* Shai Feldman, 'The New Arms Control Agenda', in Beker, *Arms Control Without Glasnost* (pp. 30–56), and Gerry Steinberg, 'Conflicting Approaches to Arms Control and CSBMS in the Middle East: Finding a Common Ground', paper presented at the IGCC conference on the Middle East multilateral talks, UCLA, June 1993. See also Yezid Sayigh, 'Middle Eastern Stability and the Proliferation of Weapons of Mass Destruction', in Efraim Karsh, Martin S. Navias and Philip Sabin (eds), *Non-Conventional Weapons Proliferation in the Middle East* (Oxford: Clarendon Press, 1993), pp. 179–204.

4   For the official Israeli view on the the arms control talks see Yossi Beilin, *A Vision of the Middle East* (Jerusalem: Israel Ministry of Foreign Affairs, December 1993), pp. 22–3. For a discussion and details of these talks in the Israeli press see Aluf Ben, 'A Preferred Company but in the Black Lists', *Ha'aretz*, 14 September, 1992; Ze'ev Schiff, 'A Test in the Red Sea', *Ha'aretz*, 8 September 1992. See also *Ha'aretz*, 20 September 1992; 21 May 1993; 10 November 1993.

5   Quoted in Feldman, 'The New Arms Control Agenda', p. 54.

6   For a reflection on Jordan's view on the arms control process see two articles by Abdullah Toukan, the head of its delegation to ACRS talks: 'A

Jordanian Perspective on Arms Control', in Eisendorf (ed.), *Arms Control and Security in the Middle East*, pp. 89–101, and 'The Middle East Peace Process, Arms Control, and Regional Security', in Spiegel and Pervin (eds), *Practical Peacemaking in the Middle East*, pp. 21–42.

7   For coverage of the meeting in Cairo see FBIS/MEA, *Daily Report*, 3 February 1994, p. 1, and 4 February 1994, pp. 3–4.

8   For coverage of the meeting in Doha see FBIS/MEA, *Daily Report*, 5 May 1994, pp. 5–6, 6 May 1994, p. 6, and 9 May, 1994, p. 5.

9   For a discussion and analysis of the tensions between Egypt and Israel during this period see Fawaz Gerges, 'Egyptian-Israeli Relations Turn Sour', *Foreign Affairs,* 74, May–June 1995, pp. 69–78. For a vehement criticism in the Israeli press of Egypt's position on NPT and the ACRS talks see Ze'ev Schiff, 'Exaggerated Demands Bordering on "Chutzpah"', *Ha'aretz*, 25 April 1995, and Ze'ev Schiff, 'Up the High Tree Again', *Ha'aretz*, 27 August 1995.

10 See BBC Summary of World Broadcasts (SWB),*The Middle East,* 9 December 1995, pp. 14–17.

11 For reports of Peres'comments on Israel's nuclear deterrent see *Ha'aretz,* 29 December 1995 and 3 January 1996.

12 At the time of going to press the parties have not yet fixed a new date for the next meeting.

Chapter 8

1   The World Bank presented two reports to the Copenhagen meeting. See World Bank, *Developing the Occupied Territories: An Investment in Peace* (November 1993) and *Economic Development and Cooperation in the Middle East and North Africa*, paper prepared by the World Bank for the regional economic development working group.

2   For details of this meeting see FBIS/MEA *Daily Report*, 20 June 1994, pp. 2–4.

3   This meeting was attended by representatives from Egypt, Israel, Jordan, the Palestinian Authority, the European Commission, the United States, Japan and France. It was the first session of the four sectoral committees, though they did report back to a plenary session. Participation in this plenary session did not reflect fully the exact composition of the monitoring committee and strictly speaking the first meeting of the monitoring committee was held prior to the REDWG plenary meeting in Bonn in January 1995.

4 It should be noted that although Saudi Arabia is a member of the Monitoring Committee it has sent a low-level representative to only one meeting.

5 A Middle East and North Africa Development Bank was one of the new institutions called for in the declaration issued at the end of the first Middle East and North Africa Economic Summit held in Casablanca on 30 October–1 November 1994. For a full text of the Casablanca Declaration see Appendix 6.

6 For a discussion of the various positions concerning the establishment of the Bank see *Financial Times*, 2 October 1995 and 27 October 1995.

7 For a full text of the Amman Declaration issued at the conclusion of the second Middle East and North Africa Economic Summit held in Amman on 29–31 October 1995 see Appendix 7.

8 This workshop was originally scheduled for November 1995 but was postponed following the assassination of Israel's Prime Minister Yitzhak Rabin.

Chapter 9

1 I. William Zartman, 'Prenegotiation: Phases and Functions', in Janice Gross-Stein (ed.), *Getting to the Table: The Process of International Prenegotiation* (Baltimore: Johns Hopkins University Press, 1989), p. 7. See also chapters by Stein and Tomlin in this book. For other discussion on the role of prenegotiation in international negotiations see Harold Saunders, 'We Need a Larger Theory of Negotiation: The Importance of Pre-negotiating Phases', *Negotiation Journal*, 1, July 1985, pp. 249–62; Jacob Bercovitch, 'International Negotiations and Conflict Management: The Importance of Prenegotiation', *Jerusalem Journal of International Relations*, 13, 1, March 1991, pp. 7–21, and Jay Rothman, 'Negotiation as Consolidation: Prenegotiation in the Israeli–Palestinian Conflict', *Jerusalem Journal of International Relations*, 13, 1, March 1991, pp. 22–43.

2 P. H. Gulliver, *Disputes and Negotiations: A Cross-Cultural Perspective* (New York: Academic Press, 1979), p. 70.

3 Bercovitch, 'International Negotiations and Conflict Management', pp. 9–14.

4 Joseph Monteville, 'The Arrow and the Olive Branch: A Case for Track Two Diplomacy', in John W. Macdonald and Diane Bendahmane (eds), *Conflict Resolution: Track Two Diplomacy* (Washington, DC: Foreign Service Institute, Department of State, 1987). The term 'Track Two

Diplomacy' was first used in William Davidson and Joseph Monteville, 'Foreign Policy according to Freud', *Foreign Policy,* 45, Winter 1981–2, pp. 145–7. For a description of the 'problem-solving workshop' approach to conflict resolution see Herbert Kelman and Steven Cohen, 'The Problem-Solving Workshop: A Social-Psychological Contribution to the Resolution of International Conflict', *Journal of Peace Research,* 13, 2, 1976, pp. 79–90, and Ronald J. Fisher, 'Prenegotiation Problem-Solving Discussions: Enhancing the Potential for Successful Negotiation', *International Journal,* 44, Spring 1989, pp. 442–74.

5 See Richard E. Benedick, 'Perspectives of a Negotiation Practitioner', in Sjostedt (ed.), *International Environmental Negotiation,* p. 238.

6 See 'The Gulf Connection', *Jerusalem Report,* 24 February 1994, pp. 26–7, 'Gulf Dreams of Trade Stream', *Guardian,* 26 October 1995, and 'Qatar–Israel Gas Accord Nearer', *Financial Times,* 28–29 October, 1995.

7 See Bruce Hurwitz, 'The Multilateral Peace Process', *Midstream,* 40, 6, 1994, p. 5.

8 See interview with Shimon Peres in 'He entered in Trauma and is Contending with a Myth', *Ha'aretz,* 24 December 1994; 'The Great Golan Gamble', *Jerusalem Report,* 28 December 1995, pp. 14–18, and *Ha'aretz,* 8 December 1995. For a blueprint of Shimon Peres' ideas for the Middle East see Peres, *The New Middle East.*

9 See Peter M. Haas, 'Introduction: Epistemic Communities and International Policy Coordination', *International Organization,* 48, 1, Winter 1992.

10 US Department of State Dispatch, 11 October, 1993, 4, 41, p. 698.

11 Many of the officials interviewed as part of the research for this book displayed very little awareness, and often total ignorance, of either previous discussions in their own area or the activities in other working groups.

12 See Klaus L. Aurisch, 'The Art of Preparing a Multilateral Conference', *Negotiation Journal,* July 1989, pp. 279–88.

13 For a discussion of potential cooperative security arrangements see Yezid Sayigh, 'The Multilateral Middle East Peace Talks: Reorganizing for Regional Security', in Spiegel and Pervin (eds), *Practical Peacemaking in the Middle East,* pp. 207–29; Ephraim Karsh and Yezid Sayigh, 'A Cooperative Approach to Arab–Israeli Security', *Survival,* 36, 1, Spring 1994, pp. 114–25 and Bowker, *Beyond Peace,* pp. 111–22.

APPENDICES

APPENDIX I: STRUCTURE OF THE MULTILATERAL TALKS

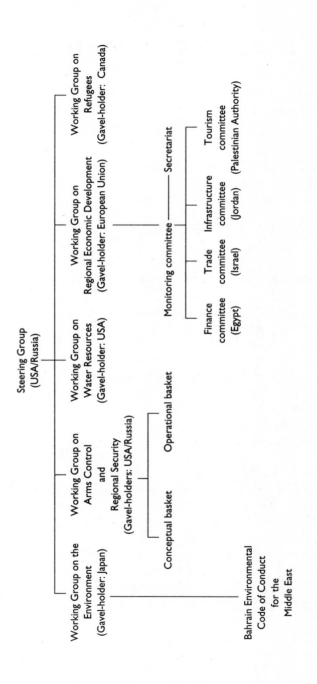

APPENDIX 2: DATES OF MEETINGS

Madrid peace conference
30 October–1 November 1991

Multilateral organizational meeting
28–29 January 1992, Moscow

Multilateral Steering Group *(co-chairs: United States and Russia)*
Round 1   27 May 1992, Lisbon
Round 2   3–4 December 1992, London
Round 3   7 July 1993, Moscow
Round 4   15-16 December 1993, Tokyo
Round 5   12–13 July 1994, Tabarka, Tunisia
Round 6   17–18 May 1995, Montreux, Switzerland

Inter-sessional meetings
9–10 February 1994, Canada
22–23 January 1995, Cairo

Multilateral working groups
Water Resources (gavel-holder: United States; co-organizers: Japan and EU)
Round 1   14–15 May 1992, Vienna
Round 2   16–17 September 1992, Washington, DC
Round 3   27–29 April 1993, Geneva
Round 4   26–28 October 1993, Beijing
Round 5   17–19 April, 1994, Muscat, Oman
Round 6   7-9 November 1194, Athens
Round 7   18–22 June 1995, Amman

Refugees (gavel-holder: Canada; co-organizers: United States, EU and Japan)
Round 1   13–15 May 1992, Ottawa
Round 2   11–12 November 1992, Ottawa
Round 3   11–13 May 1993, Oslo
Round 4   12–14 October 1993, Tunis
Round 5   10–12 May 1994, Cairo
Round 6   13–14 December 1994, Antalya, Turkey
Round 7   11–14 December 1995, Geneva

Arms Control and Regional Security (gavel-holders: United States and Russia)
Round 1   11-14 May 1992, Washington, DC
Round 2   15–17 September 1992, Moscow
Round 3   18–20 May 1993, Washington, DC
Round 4   2–4 November 1993, Moscow
Round 5   3–5 May, 1994, Doha, Qatar
Round 6   12–15 December 1994, Tunis

Conceptual basket
Meeting 1   30 January–3 February 1994, Cairo
Meeting 2   12–14 October 1994, Paris
Meeting 3   29 May–1 June 1995, Helsinki

Operational basket
Meeting 1   20–24 March 1994, Antalya, Turkey
Meeting 2   7–9 November 1994, Dead Sea, Jordan
Meeting 3   4–6 April 1995, Antalya, Turkey

Environment (gavel-holder: Japan: co-organizers: United States and EU)
Round 1   18–19 May 1992, Tokyo
Round 2   26–27 September 1992, The Hague
Round 3   24–25 May 1993, Tokyo
Round 4   15–16 November 1993, Cairo
Round 5   6–7 April 1994, The Hague
Round 6   25–26 October 1994, Manama, Bahrain
Round 7   18-22 June 1995, Amman

Regional Economic Development (gavel-holder: EU; co-organizers: United States and Japan)

Round 1   11–12 May 1992, Brussels
Round 2   29–30 October 1992, Paris
Round 3   4–5 May 1993, Rome
Round 4   8–9 November 1993, Copenhagen
Round 5   15–16 June 1994, Rabat
Round 6   18–19 January 1995, Bonn
Round 7   12 March 1996, Amman

REDWG Monitoring Committee
Meeting 1   17 January 1995, Bonn
Meeting 2   26 June 1995, Cairo
Meeting 3   15 December 1995, Brussels

Finance committee
Meeting 1   5 December 1994, Cairo
Meeting 2   17 January 1995, Bonn
Meeting 3   1–2 April 1995, Amman
Meeting 4   16–17 May 1995, Cairo
Meeting 4   7 August 1995, Amman

Trade committee
Meeting 1   5 December 1994, Cairo
Meeting 2   17 January 1995, Bonn
Meeting 3   18 April 1995, Cairo
Meeting 4   25 June 1995, Cairo
Meeting 5   14–15 December 1995, Geneva

Tourism committee
Meeting 1   5 December 1994, Cairo
Meeting 2   17 January 1995, Bonn
Meeting 3   14–15 March 1995, Cairo
Meeting 4   11–12 July 1995, Haifa

Infrastructure committee
Meeting 1   5 December 1994, Cairo
Meeting 2   17 January 1995, Bonn
Meeting 3   6–7 June 1995, Amman

APPENDIX 3: THE BAHRAIN ENVIRONMENTAL CODE OF CONDUCT FOR THE MIDDLE EAST

The Multilateral Working Group on the Environment of the Middle East peace process initiated at Madrid in October 1991,

Based upon the discussions which have taken place in the Cairo Consultative Group,

Reaffirming the role of the multilateral talks in promoting confidence-building and cooperation among the regional parties in the field of the environment,

Noting relevant international Declarations and instruments on the environment and sustainable development; and recognizing, in particular, the Rio Declaration on Environment and Development and Agenda 21 adopted in 1992,

Recognizing that, in view of the inseparable relationship between humans and their environment, all aspects of the human environment, be they natural or man-made, are essential to the well-being and the enjoyment of basic human life,

Convinced of the need for the protection and conservation of the environment and natural resources in the region,

Recognizing that in view of transboundary effects of many environmental problems, each party needs to take into consideration effects upon other parties in pursuing its own developmental and environmental policy,

Also recognizing the need for passing on to the future generations of the region a safe, sound and healthy environment as well as the fruits of economic development,

Recognizing the unique environmental characteristics to the Middle East,

Declares as follows:

Principles

1. The regional parties proclaim the following principles:

(1) Natural resources of the region should be utilized on a sustainable basis, and unique environmental resources to the region should be preserved.

(2) The parties will strive for a fair and just utilization and coordinated management policies of the shared natural resources in the region.

(3) The parties have the right to exploit their own resources pursuant to their own environmental and developmental policies, and the responsibility to ensure that activities within their jurisdiction or control do not cause damage to the environment of other parties.

(4) The parties have the responsibility to avoid activities of adverse effect and risks to the environmental security in the region.

(5) Economic development should be in harmony with the protection and conservation of the environment, including preservation of ecological balance and safety of human health and well-being. The parties will promote cooperation in the protection and conservation of the environment.

(6) A comprehensive, just and lasting peace in the region, development and environmental protection are interdependent and indivisible.

(7) Regional parties will cooperate and seek the cooperation of other parties in the essential task of eradicating poverty as an indispensable requirement for sustainable development, in order to decrease the disparities in standards of living and better meet the needs of the people in the region.

(8) Environmental issues are best handled with the participation of all concerned citizens and social sectors, at the relevant level. The parties shall facilitate and encourage public awareness and participation by making information widely available.

Guidelines

2. In order to pursue policies in accordance with the Principles, the regional parties should:

(a) Enact effective environmental legislation. Environmental standards, management objectives and priorities should reflect the state of the environment in the Middle East, paying due consideration to geographical, topographical and meteorological conditions as well as regional environmental problems such as water, air and marine pollution, waste management, desertification and nature conservation.

(b) Develop and use environmental management tools such as environmental impact assessment, environmental risk management and monitoring systems, for domestic as well as transboundary impacts; in case of projects with possible transboundary effects, all regional parties involved should endeavour to cooperate on an environment impact assessment.

(c) Strive for capacity building and human resource development, through environmental training and education.

(d) Facilitate and encourage public awareness to broaden the basis for enlightened opinions and responsible conduct by individuals, enterprises and communities in protecting and improving the environment.

(e) Coordinate their environmental policies with one another and cooperate in protecting the over-all environment in the region in good faith and in a spirit of partnership.

(f) Cooperate in promoting appropriate technology and capability to tackle environmental issues by joint projects, joint research and other activities where appropriate; facilitate the transfer of technology, know-how, and information; notify one another of environmental situations that have regional or transboundary impacts.

(g) Endeavour to promote the internalization of environmental costs and the use of economic instruments, taking into account the approach that the polluter should, in principle, bear the cost of pollution, with due regard to the public interest and without distorting international trade and investment.

(h) Resolve all their environmental disputes peacefully and by appropriate means in accordance with the UN Charter and in conformity with relevant provisions of international law and declarations.

Joint actions

3. The regional parties will join forces for the environmental protection and conservation and begin to work in the following fields:

Water: Protection of water quality should be given a top priority. Low precipitation in the region makes it extremely important to maintain the quality of surface and ground water for both economic activities and human consumption.

Marine and coastal environment: The sea surfaces of the Middle East are both economic and environmental assets for the regional parties. They are most vulnerable to pollution, from land base sources and maritime activities in particular. It is essential to apply advanced standards to eliminate these sources of pollution, and to cooperate in all possible ways to assure protection of coasts and biodiversity in waters.

Air: Economic activities particularly in the industrial, energy and transport sectors are main sources for air pollution in the Middle East. Measures to prevent the degradation of air quality need to be taken.

Waste management: With rising living standards and increasing economic activity, the regional parties may have to dispose of increasing amounts of waste in the future. The parties will need to: minimize waste, enact effective regulations for proper treatment, recycling and protection measures, and ensure safe waste disposal within agreed safety measures and emergency preparedness arrangements in the region. Sewage, as a potential important resource, should be collected and treated to be reused for various purposes.

Desertification: The Middle East region is among those threatened by land degradation including desertification, and preventive measures are urgently needed. To combat desertification and mitigate the effects of drought in particular, effective cooperative actions are indispensable.

A regional framework

4. The parties recognize the need for regional cooperation in the field of environment in the Middle East. The parties will work towards the development of an appropriate framework for regional cooperation in the environ-

mental area. Towards this end, it is important that the regional parties provide timely and early notification and relevant information on environmental situations that have regional impacts on potentially affected parties.

Extra-regional assistance
5. The extra-regional parties, including international organizations, are invited to assist the regional parties in their endeavours to achieve the goals and objectives of this Code.

Periodic review
6. This Code should be brought to the attention of all concerned parties so that they assume their share of responsibility, individually or jointly to ensure that the objectives of the Code are met. The Parties will periodically assess the effectiveness of the Code of Conduct and revise it as appropriate.

This document was endorsed by the Middle East peace process environment working group on 25 October 1994 in Bahrain.

APPENDIX 4: REGIONAL ECONOMIC DEVELOPMENT WORKING GROUP, COPENHAGEN ACTION PLAN, NOVEMBER 1993

In each section, the sponsor is given in the left-hand column and the subject or project in the right-hand column.

Communications and transport

France	Workshop of transport officials from the region
EU	Regional workshops on technical problems of transport and communications
EU	Engineering study, road from Amman to Jericho and Jerusalem
EU	Pre-feasibility study, road from Aqaba–Eilat to Egypt
EU	Workshop of civil aviation officials

Energy

EU/Austria	Study of electricity grid interconnection
EU/Austria	Workshop on electricity grid interconnection
EU	Review of existing studies of hydroelectric power plant on the Dead Sea

Tourism

Japan	Workshop on regional tourism
EU	European tour operators to be associated with above workshop
USA	American tour operators to be associated with above workshop
Switzerland	Regional training in hotel management and tourism in association with the private sector

Agriculture

Spain	Study on agricultural development in the region (food self-sufficiency and regional trade)
EU	Mission to identify areas of veterinary medicine networks in animal health and livestock improvement, joint vaccination
EU	Workshop of senior veterinary officials

Financial markets and investment

UK	Conference on financial markets
UK	Study on greater cooperation among stock markets
EU	Workshop on the business, legal and regulatory environment for the private sector
EU/Switzerland	European and regional business conference to promote joint ventures

Trade

Germany	Study on regional cooperation in trade of goods and services
Germany	Follow-up study to above
EU/Switzerland	Workshop on the administrative simplification of the movement of goods

Training

USA	Regional business development round table
USA	Regional 'Educating Workforce 2000': a regional symposium on education
USA	Regional seminar on animal health in the Middle East
USA	Regional workshop on water management systems
Germany	Study of vocational education and technical training in the region
Germany	Workshop based on results of above study
World Bank	Network of regional training institutes organized by EDI

Networks

EU	Workshop on EU and regional cooperation among municipalities
EU	Workshop on EU and regional cooperation among universities

Bibliography

Canada	Updated review of the literature on economic cooperation in the Middle East
Canada	Possible inter-sessional activity based on above

APPENDIX 5: COPENHAGEN ACTION PLAN, UPDATE – DECEMBER 1995

In each section, the sponsor is given in the left-hand column, the subject or project in the middle column, and dates or other notes on status in the right-hand column.

Communications and transport (shepherd: France)

EU/France	Workshop of transport officials from the region	3–6 May 1994, Paris
EU	Workshop on regional road infrastructure	10–12 October 1994, Cairo
EU/France	Workshop on regional railways	May 1995, Paris
EU/France	Workshop on port and maritime sector	March 1995, Marseille
France	Workshop on road transport regulation	25–27 October 1994, Paris
EU, USA, ICAO, France	Workshop of civil aviation officials	4–7 April 1995, Toulouse
USA	Feasibility study of regional navigation and air traffic control	8 January 1995 Washington, DC
France	Feasibility study of Gaza port	Ongoing
EU	Middle East regional transport study	Starting end 1995
EU	Pre-feasibility study on railway links between Israel and Jordan	Planned
EU	Workshop on Middle East traffic corridors	October 1995

Energy (shepherd: Austria)

EU/Austria	Study on electricity grid interconnection	Final report March 1995
EU	Review of existing studies of hydroelectric power plant on Dead Sea-Red Sea and Mediterranean	Completed June 1994
Italy	Feasibility study of Egypt–Gaza pipeline	Started end 1993; ongoing

Tourism (shepherd: Japan)

Japan	Workshop on regional cooperation in tourism (No. 1)	6–7 February 1994, Cairo
Japan	Workshop on regional cooperation in tourism (No. 2)	27–28 November 1994, Cairo
Japan	Workshop on regional cooperation in tourism (No. 3)	28–30 March 1995
Japan	Seminar on policies for promotion of small–medium enterprises related to tourism	16–29 January 1995, Cairo
EU	Workshop of European tour operators and regional tourism officials	23–25 January 1995, Aqaba
USA	Workshop of American tour operators and regional tourism officials	28–29 September 1994, Cairo
Japan	Technical assistance to the REDWG sectoral committee on tourism; establishment of a regional tourism board	Established at Amman economic summit
Switzerland	Feasibility study on regional training of hotel and tourism personnel	Completed

Agriculture (shepherd: Spain)

Spain	Study on agricultural development in the region (food self-sufficiency and regional trade)	Completed September 1995

Spain	Workshop on plant protection	Planned
Spain	Creation of an agency for regional cooperation in agriculture and livestock	Planned
EU	Preparation of regional veterinary project feasibility study Provision of technical assistance to Palestinian veterinary authority	1995
EU	Workshop of senior veterinary officials	12–14 December 1994, Cairo

Financial markets and investments (shepherd: UK)

UK	Seminar on financial markets	28–29 April 1994, London
UK	Study on greater cooperation among stock markets	Completed June 1994
EU/UK	Preparation of programme to reduce barriers to inward investment	Under discussion
EU/World Bank	Workshop on the role of the private sector in public infrastructure	30 May–2 June 1995, Istanbul

Trade (shepherd: Germany)

Germany	Study on regional cooperation in trade for goods and services	Completed
Germany	Study on opportunities and risks of closer economic cooperation in the Near East	30 July 1995
EU/Switzerland	Workshop on the administrative simplification of the movement of goods	Presented at Amman summit
Sweden	Seminar on trade policy and the interlinkages between different trade agreement areas	Initiated 1995
EU	Trade barriers survey in the Middle East	Presented at Amman summit

| USA | Technical assistance to the REDWG sectoral committee on trade for the establishment of a regional business council | Announced at Amman summit |

Health (shepherd: Italy)

Italy	Health technology assessment	Ongoing
Italy/UNICEF	Training needs for Palestinian health managers; creation of a health services management unit	Started January 1995
Italy/UNWRA	Planning a central public health laboratory in West Bank	Planned

Training (shepherd: United States)

USA	Regional workshop on water management systems in conjunction with the water working group	4–16 June 1994, Orlando
US	Regional seminar on animal health in the Middle East	17–20 April 1994 Sharm El Sheikh, Egypt
Germany	Regional study on labour-market-orientated training	Ongoing
Germany	Conference on labour-market-orientated training	June 1995, Heidelberg
India	Pre-feasibility study for a technical centre in Gaza and Jericho to create trainers for the region	Planned
World Bank	Network of regional training institutes organized by EDI	Planned

Networks and information (shepherd: EU)

| EU | Peace-URBS | Ongoing workshop, 6–9 March 1995, Aqaba |

EU	Peace–CAMPUS	Ongoing workshop 6–9 March, 1995 Aqaba
EC	Peace–MEDIA	Ongoing workshop 6–9 March 1995, Aqaba
Canada	Literature on economic cooperation in the Middle East	August 1994
Canada	Follow-up of the above on Egypt	June 1995
EU	MEPPIB (Middle East Peace Process Information Bank)	Ongoing

APPENDIX 6: THE FIRST MIDDLE EAST/ NORTH AFRICA ECONOMIC SUMMIT: THE CASABLANCA DECLARATION

1. At the invitation of His Majesty King Hassan II of Morocco and with the support and endorsement of Presidents Bill Clinton of the United States and Boris Yeltsin of the Russian Federation, the representatives of 61 countries and 1,114 business leaders from all regions of the world, gathered for a Middle East/ North Africa Economic Summit in Casablanca from October 30 to November 1, 1994. The participants paid tribute to His Majesty, King Hassan II, in his capacity as President and Host of the Conference and praised his role in promoting dialogue and understanding between the parties in the Middle East conflict. They also expressed their appreciation to the Government and people of Morocco for their hospitality and efforts to ensure the success of the Summit.

2. The Summit leaders feel united behind the vision that brought them to Casablanca, that of a comprehensive peace and a new partnership of business and government dedicated to furthering peace between Arabs and Israelis.

3. Government and business leaders entered into this new partnership with a deeper understanding of their mutual dependence and common goals. Business leaders recognized that governments should continue to forge peace agreements and create foundations and incentives for trade and investment. They further recognize the responsibility of the private sector to apply its new international influence to advance the diplomacy of peace in the Middle East and beyond. Governments affirmed the indispensability of the private sector in marshalling, quickly, adequate resources to demonstrate the tangible benefits of peace. Together, they pledged to show that business can do business and contribute to peace as well; indeed, to prove that profitability contributes mightily to the economic scaffolding for a durable peace.

4. The Summit commended the historic political transformation of the Region as a consequence of significant steps towards a just, lasting and comprehensive peace, based on U.N. Security Council Resolutions 242 and

338, a process that began with the 1979 Treaty of Peace between Egypt and Israel and enlarged dramatically by the Madrid Peace conference, three years ago. That process has borne fruit in the Israel–Palestine Liberation Organization Declaration of Principles. The recent signing of the Treaty of Peace between Israel and Jordan gave a new dimension to the process. The decisions of Morocco and Tunisia to establish, respectively, liaison offices and liaison channels with Israel, constituted another new positive development. These accomplishments and the next stages of rapid movement toward a comprehensive peace in the region, including Syria and Lebanon, need to be powerfully reinforced by solid economic growth and palpable improvement of the life and security of the peoples of this region. The Summit stressed that Syria and Lebanon have an important role to play in the development of the region. The Summit expressed a strong hope that they will soon be able to join the regional economic effort.

5. In this connection, the participants noted that the urgent need for economic development of the West Bank and Gaza Strip requires special attention from the international community, both public and private, in order to support the Israel–Palestine Liberation Organization Declaration of Principles and subsequent implementing agreements to enable the Palestinian people to participate on equal bases in the regional development and cooperation. They stressed the equal importance of moving ahead on Jordanian–Israeli projects as well as on cooperative projects between Israel and Jordan in order to advance the Jordanian–Israeli Treaty of Peace.

6. The participants recognized the economic potential of the Middle East and North Africa and explored how best to accelerate the development of the Region and overcome, as soon as possible, obstacles, including boycotts and all barriers to trade and investment. All agreed that there is a need to promote increased investment from inside and outside the Region. They noted that such investment requires free movement of goods, capital and labour across borders in accordance with market forces, technical cooperation based on mutual interest, openness to the international economy and appropriate institutions to promote economic interaction. They also noted that the free flow of ideas and increased dialogue, especially among the business communities in the Region, will strengthen economic activity. In this context, the participants noted favourably the decision of the Council for Cooperation of

the Gulf States regarding the lifting of the secondary and the tertiary aspects of the boycott of Israel.

7. Based on the agreements between Israel and the PLO, it is important that the borders of the Palestinian Territories be kept open for labour, tourism and trade to allow the Palestinian Authority, in partnership with its neighbours, the opportunity to build a viable economy in peace.

8. The participants paid tribute to the multilateral negotiations initiated in Moscow in 1992 which have significantly advanced the objectives of the peace process. The governments represented at Casablanca will examine ways to enhance the role and activities of the multilateral negotiations, including examining regional institutions which address economic, humanitarian and security issues. The participants noted that the progresses made in the peace process should go along with a serious consideration of the socio-economic disparities in the Region and require to address the idea of security in the Region in all its dimensions: social, economic and political. In this context, they agreed that these issues need to be addressed within the framework of a global approach encompassing socio-economic dimensions, safety and welfare of Individuals and Nations of the Region.

9. The participants recognized that there must be an ongoing process to translate the deliberations of Casablanca into concrete steps to advance the twin goals of peace and economic development and to institutionalize the new partnership between governments and the business community.

To this end:

(a) The governments represented at Casablanca and private sector representatives stated their intention to take the following steps:

— Build the foundations for a Middle East and North Africa Economic Community which involves, at a determined stage, the free flow of goods, capital and labour throughout the Region.
— Taking into account the recommendations of the regional parties during the meeting of the sub-committee on finances of the REDWG monitoring committee, this sub-committee will call for a group of

experts to examine the different options for a funding mechanism including the creation of a Middle East and North Africa Development Bank. This group of experts will report on its progress and conclusions within six months in the light of the follow-on Summit to the Casablanca Conference. The funding mechanism would include appropriate bodies to promote dialogue on economic reform, regional cooperation, technical assistance and long-term development planning.

– Establish a regional Tourist Board to facilitate tourism and promote the Middle East and North Africa as a unique and attractive tourist destination.

– Encourage the establishment of a private sector Regional Chamber of Commerce and Business Council to facilitate intra-regional trade relations. Such organizations will be instrumental in solidifying ties between the private and public sectors of the various economies.

(b) The participants also intend to create the following mechanisms to implement these understandings and embody the new public–private collaboration:

– A Steering Committee, comprised of government representatives, including those represented in the Steering Committee of the multilateral group of the peace process, will be entrusted with the task of following up all issues arising out of the REDWG and other multilateral working groups. The Steering Committee will meet within one month following the Casablanca Summit to consider follow-on mechanisms. The Committee will consult widely and regularly with the private sector.

– An executive Secretariat to assist the Steering Committee, located in Morocco, will work for the enhancement of the new economic development pattern, thus contributing to the consolidation of the global security in the Region. The Secretariat will assist in the organization of a Regional Chamber of Commerce and a Business Council. It will work to advance the public–private partnership by promoting projects, sharing data, promoting contacts and fostering private sector investment in the region. The Secretariat will assist in the implementation of the various bodies referred to in the present Declaration. The

Steering Committee will be responsible for the funding arrangements, with the support of the private sector.

10. The participants welcomed the establishment of a Middle East/North Africa Economic Strategy group by the Council on Foreign Relations. This private sector group will recommend strategies for regional economic cooperation and ways to overcome obstacles to trade and private investment. It will operate in close association with the Secretariat and submit its recommendations to the Steering Committee.

11. The participants also welcomed the intention of the World Economic Forum to form a business interaction group that will foster increased contacts and exchanges among business communities and submit its recommendations to the Steering Committee.

12. The participants in the Casablanca Summit pledged to transform this event into lasting institutional and individual ties that will provide a better life for the peoples of the Middle East and North Africa. They resolved that the collaboration of the public and private sectors that constituted the singularity of the Casablanca Summit will serve as a milestone in the historic destiny that is now playing itself out in the Middle East/North Africa Region.

13. The participants expressed their appreciation to the Council on Foreign Relations and to the World Economic Forum for their substantive contribution to the organization of the Casablanca Summit.

14. The participants expressed their intention to meet again in Amman, Jordan, in the first half of 1995 for a second Middle East/North Africa Economic Summit, to be hosted by His Majesty King Hussein.

APPENDIX 7: THE SECOND MIDDLE EAST/ NORTH AFRICA ECONOMIC SUMMIT: THE AMMAN DECLARATION

On October 29–31, 1995, the second Middle East/North Africa Economic Summit was held in Amman, Jordan under the patronage of His Majesty King Hussein bin Talal. The Summit, co-sponsored by the United States and the Russian Federation, with the support of the European Union, Canada, and Japan, brought together government and business leaders from the Middle East and North Africa, Europe, the Americas, and Asia. Summit participants thank His Majesty King Hussein for his able leadership and for the extraordinary efforts by the Hashemite Kingdom of Jordan to make this Summit a success. The participants also expressed their appreciation for the partnership of the World Economic Forum, which assisted so ably in organizing this event.

The goals of the Summit were to facilitate the expansion of private sector investment in the region, to cement a public–private partnership which will ensure that end, and to work to enhance regional cooperation and development. In this spirit, business leaders from the Middle East, North Africa and other regions were able to conclude a number of significant commercial and business transactions at the Summit that will help augment the productive capacity of the region and contribute to its broad-based economic development. These ventures involved projects in the fields of tourism, telecommunications, and transportation. Reflecting this public–private partnership, a number of these ventures will benefit from government guarantees, technical assistance, and other support from the international community.

Government representatives conducted a series of negotiations over the past year on institutional arrangements as called for in the Casablanca Declaration which would help underpin the peace process. In this respect, the following agreements have been reached:

A Bank for Economic Cooperation and Development

A Bank for Economic Cooperation and Development in the Middle East and North Africa will be established in Cairo. The Bank as described in its draft articles will be structured to promote development of the private sector, support regional infrastructure projects, and provide a Forum to promote regional economic cooperation. The Task Force will finalize its negotiations by December 31, 1995 and will continue to explore proposals for the creation of a project preparation and financial intermediation facility. Those wishing to join the Bank will begin their national ratification processes thereafter. Others wish to leave open the option of joining the Bank at a later date, in light of the evolution of institutional arrangements and other developments. The Economic Summit will review this issue at its next meeting.

Regional Tourism Board

The establishment of a Regional Tourism Board, the Middle East–Mediterranean Travel and Tourism Association, to facilitate tourism and promote the region as a unique and attractive tourist destination. The Board will include both public and private representatives.

Regional Business Council

The establishment of a Regional Business Council to promote cooperation and trade among the private sectors of the countries of the region.

Economic Summit Executive Secretariat

The formal inauguration of the Economic Summit Executive Secretariat, which is located in Rabat and works to advance the public–private partnership, promoting contacts, sharing data, and fostering private sector investment in the region. The participants expressed their appreciation to the Moroccan Government for its contribution to this effort, and confirmed their support for its ongoing activities.

Regional Economic and Development Working Group, Monitoring Committee Secretariat

As a complement to the regional institutions called for at Casablanca, the Steering Group of the Multilateral Peace Negotiations has decided to establish the Regional Economic and Development Working Group, REDWG, Monitoring Committee Secretariat as a permanent regional economic institution to be based in Amman. All participating parties have agreed that this institution will promote and strengthen regional economic cooperation in the Middle East and North Africa. The regional parties strongly recommend that the Secretariat's activities will cover the range of sectors within the REDWG Monitoring Committee's work, i.e. infrastructure, tourism, trade, finance, and areas within the Copenhagen Plan of Action. The core parties in close consultation with the European Union and other members of the Monitoring Committee undertake to finalize the appropriate document on the structure and operational functions of this institution, which will be submitted to the next meeting of the REDWG plenary, with a view to the commencement of the institution's activities in the first half of 1996. This REDWG plenary will consider the matter, take appropriate action, and report to the upcoming meeting of the Multilateral Steering Group.

The participants at the Summit expressed their strong support for continued progress in the peace process begun at Madrid exactly four years ago, and the importance of achieving a comprehensive peace. Participants took particular note of the advances made in the past year. Summit participants welcomed the signing of the Israeli–Palestinian Interim Agreement in the West Bank and Gaza Strip, and took favourable note of the significant progress made in implementing the Treaty of Peace between Agreement in the West Bank and Gaza Strip, and took favourable note of the significant progress made in implementing the Treaty of Peace between Israel and Jordan.

The Summit welcomed the decision to organize in Paris, in December 1995, the Ministerial Conference on Economic Assistance for the Palestinians. The Summit also took note of the positive contribution made towards peace by multilateral working groups. While welcoming an increasingly positive atmosphere of openness in the region, the Summit recognized that the circle of peace needs to be widened. Participants expressed the hope that peace agreements between Israel and Syria and Israel and Lebanon would be concluded as soon as possible.

The Summit welcomed significant steps taken by regional parties to the Taba Declaration and by the GCC with regard to lifting the boycott on Israel, and expressed its support for additional efforts to end the boycott.

The participants at the Summit declared their intent to implement as soon as possible the understandings reached in Amman. With respect to commercial activities, the business representatives reaffirmed their intention to follow through on the commercial ventures reached here and to explore new opportunities to expand trade and investment in the region. On the part of governments, the officials attending the Summit declared their intention to support the activities of the private sector, most particularly by getting the new institutions established in Amman up and running as soon as possible. The participants also welcomed the measures taken by regional parties to open their economies and join the global economy.

To continue such a process whose blueprint and institutions have been established here, in Amman today, two brotherly countries announced their interest to host the next session of the MENA Summit. They are Qatar and Egypt. His Majesty King Hussein conducted the necessary consultations with the distinguished representatives of the two brotherly states, as well as with other interested parties. He gladly announced that Qatar has graciously conceded its offer to host the next summit in favour of Egypt, who will host it. And it has been agreed by all, including Jordan, the present host, as well as Egypt and others, that Qatar will be the venue of the Middle East/North Africa Economic Summit in 1997.

Chatham House Papers  THE ROYAL INSTITUTE OF INTERNATIONAL AFFAIRS

Recent title from Chatham House

Hussein J. Agha
and
Ahmad S. Khalidi

SYRIA AND IRAN
Rivalry and Cooperation

Contents

• The roots of the
Syrian–Iranian alliance

• Critical states
in the evolution of
the alliance

• Iran, Syria and
the Arab–Israeli peace
process

• After Madrid:
local and regional factors

• Relations with the
United States and Russia

• Military, economic
and domesic factors

• Conclusion:
a limited alliance

ISBN 1 85567 235 9 (pbk)

Syrian–Iranian relations have been characterized by an unusual combination of political rivalry and pragmatic cooperation. This study of one of the least comprehended aspects of Middle East politics focuses on the development of this alliance of convenience within the context of the Arab–Israeli conflict and the Middle East peace process.

The volume starts with an account of the origins of this apparently puzzling relationship, and considers the primary factors that have helped to sustain it over the past decade and a half. The authors examine the political, military and economic aspects of the alliance and their regional significance. They assess the attitude of both parties to a Middle East settlement and the impact that such a settlement may have on the future of the relationship.

The authors

Hussein J. Agha and Ahmad S. Khalidi are Associate Fellows of the Middle East Programme at the Royal Institute of International Affairs

July 1995   RIIA/Pinter   Price £11.99

Chatham House Papers  THE ROYAL INSTITUTE OF INTERNATIONAL AFFAIRS

Recent title from Chatham House

Paul Cornish

THE ARMS TRADE AND EUROPE

Contents

ISBN 1 85567 285 5 (pbk)

As the world arms market continues to contract, competition for remaining contracts intensifies, and the advantage in the market place is shifting increasingly towards the buyer. Sensing this shift, buyers are more questioning of Western values such as universal human rights and democracy, and more confident in rejecting attempts to link such values with arms and technology deals. Something like a free market in weapons and military equipment has arrived.

The European Union has taken a leading part in post-Cold War attempts to regulate the international arms market. This study draws attention to important differences, as far as the EU is concerned, between trade in finished weapons and trade in manufacturing technology. It examines west European attempts to manage both sides of conventional defence-related trade and evaluates the current obstacles to effective multilateral coordination and regulation.

Dr Paul Cornish is a Senior Research Fellow in the International Security Programme at the Royal Institute of International Affairs.

November 1995   RIIA/Pinter   Price £10.99

Chatham House Papers  THE ROYAL INSTITUTE OF INTERNATIONAL AFFAIRS

Recent title from Chatham House

Michael Cox

US FOREIGN POLICY AFTER THE COLD WAR
Superpower Without a Mission?

Contents

- The constrained superpower?

- From geopolitics to geo-economics? Competing in a global economy

- Planning for the next war: restructuring defence

- Strategic alliance or cold peace? Managing post-Communist Russia

- Atlantic rift? The United States and Europe after the Cold War

- The United States meets the Pacific century

- Whatever happened to the Third World?

ISBN 1 85567 221 9 (pbk)

'... the most important book to date about post-Cold War American foreign policy ... required reading for anyone trying to understand the international role of the last remaining superpower at the close of the century.' – *Benjamin Schwarz, formerly RAND*

'A splendid account of recent US foreign policy ... shows both the surprising continuities after the Cold War as well as the dramatic shifts from geopolitics to geo-economics ... there is no better book to read on Clinton's foreign policies.' – *Professor Melvyn Leffler, University of Virginia*

'... a clear-headed and thoughtful assessment ... Cox has looked well beyond the headlines to produce the most comprehensive and far-sighted study of this confusing topic so far.' – *Martin Walker, US Bureau Chief, The Guardian*

'No one understands American foreign policy better than Michael Cox, as he demonstrates once again in this informed and stimulating study.' – *Ronald Steel, Professor of International Relations, University of Southern California*

Michael Cox is a member of the Department of International Politics at the University of Wales in Aberystwyth, and Associate Research Fellow at the Royal Institute of International Affairs.

November 1995   RIIA/Pinter   Price £11.99